FARSON, Richard Evans. Birthrights. Macmillan, 1974. 248p 73-6487. 6.96. ISBN 0-02-537170-3. C.I.P.

Farson, a cofounder of the Western Behavioral Science Institute, offers a dynamic and systematic analysis of what he characterizes as "ageism" in our society as it relates to one end of the continuum — that of children. The book attempts to address, in a clear and articulate exposition, those facets of society which impact and impinge upon the child, ranging from socialization and citizenship to economy and justice, stressing the interrelationship between and among these critical areas as well as pointing up the need to rethink the context from which changes may be effected, i.e., reconceptualizations of family, community, social, political, and judicial processes. Farson writes simply and clearly, and, while not as mindful of stated referenced documentation as might be desirable, sets forth innumerable reference listings grouped in order of appearance by chapter. This book is timely in that a Child Advocacy Movement is visibly progressing in this country. While cognizant of the critical need to address discrimination against children and to restore to them a full measure of human rights, Farson appears to find a more viable mechanism to achieve this objective in broad, humane reform, rather than an incremental and limited, at-risk population approach. General readership.

Birthrights

BIRTHRIGHTS

Richard Farson

Macmillan Publishing Co., Inc.
NEW YORK
Collier Macmillan Publishers
LONDON

Macmillan Publishing Co., Inc.
866 Third Avenue, New York, N.Y. 10022
Collier-Macmillan Canada Ltd.

Library of Congress Catalog Card Number: 73-6487

First Printing 1974

LIBRARY OF CONGRESS CATALOGING IN PUBLICATION DATA

Farson, Richard Evans, date
Birthrights.

Includes bibliographical references.
1. Children's rights. 2. Parent and child.
3. Children in the United States. I. Title.
HQ789.F37 301.43'14 73-6487
ISBN 0-02-537170-3

Printed in the United States of America

FOR

Lisa,
Clark,
Joel,
Ashley,
Jeremy

CHILD—N. child, infant, babe, baby, little one, kid (slang), moppet, bairn (Scot.), bambino, bantling, bud, chick, chit, nestling, shaver, sprat, tad, tot, tyke; whelp, youngster, cherub, elf, papoose (N. Amer. Indian), pickaninny, urchin; neonate, suckling, nursling, weanling; orphan; minor (law), ward; foundling, changeling, waif; brat, enfant terrible (F.), oaf, ragamuffin, ugly duckling.

Acknowledgments

I find it simply impossible to acknowledge adequately the many contributions of family, friends, colleagues, teachers, students, editors, and typists who helped in the writing of this book, let alone all the civil libertarians, social philosophers, and child advocates throughout history who provided the intellectual underpinnings of the arguments presented here. Rather than try to acknowledge all of them I hope that they will understand if, as a means of special recognition, I were to acknowledge only one person by name—my research assistant, Jill Soderholm. Jill worked tirelessly finding books, researching obscure articles, handling correspondence, organizing files, investigating children's programs, interviewing child advocates, contributing ideas, editing rough drafts and performing many other tasks, especially during the long period of twenty-hour work days during which we were readying the final manuscript to meet the publishing deadline. Without her help the book might never have been written, and I am deeply grateful to her.

Contents

Birthrights

1

The Politics of Childhood

A common error made by children reciting the pledge of allegiance to the flag is, ". . . one nation, under God, invisible . . ." There is truth in the error. To them the nation is indeed invisible. Excluded from almost every area of life in America, they have no opportunity to see it. Moreover, children are invisible to the nation. Segregated, ignored, impotent.

Our world is not a good place for children. Every institution in our society severely discriminates against them. We all come to feel that it is either natural or necessary to cooperate in that discrimination. Unconsciously, we carry out the will of a society which holds a limited and demeaned view of children and which refuses to recognize their right to full humanity.

To the extent that we spend time with children, we spend it protecting, teaching, controlling, and disciplining them in the service of institutions which care little about their best interests. We must continually protect our children from physical danger, such as speeding automobiles. We serve oppressive compulsory schools by guaranteeing that children make progress toward becoming standardized educational products. We control them so that in stores or restaurants (almost all of which are designed only for adults) children don't act like children. We discipline children so that they will blindly obey adult authority whenever it is encountered.

Our society's ideal child is cute (entertaining to adults), well-behaved (doesn't bother adults), and bright (capable of early admission to his parents' favorite college). Efforts of parents to produce these traits have so inhibited children that neither adults nor children can see their remarkable potentialities.

This may change. The civil rights movement and the various liberation efforts which it has ignited have alerted us to the many forms oppression takes in our society. As a result, we are now seeing the children as we have not seen them before—powerless, dominated, ignored, invisible. And we are beginning to see the necessity for children's liberation.

The move for children's rights comes from the realization on the part of lawyers and judges, psychiatrists and educators, social workers and political reformers, parents and children that freedom and democracy are not the rights of adults only. Concerned people in every institution are becoming aware of the heavy reliance on power and authority by which adults impose excessive and arbitrary controls on children. In the developing consciousness of a civilization which has for four hundred years gradually excluded children from the world of adults there is the dawning recognition that children must have the right to full participation in society, that they must be valued for themselves, not just as potential adults.[1]

Liberating children, giving them equality, may seem to violate the fairly recent realization that children are not simply miniature adults, that childhood is a special time of life with special qualities and problems. After all, never before in history have psychologists and parents and teachers had so much "understanding" of children. The trouble is that understanding developed in a context in which children are continually subjugated is suspect in itself and in any case is insufficient to provide for children in a world that is organized against them. Increased understanding has not been coupled with increased rights. As a consequence, children's rights have actually diminished, for we have simply replaced ignorant domination of children with sophisticated domination.

If the advocacy for children's rights should succeed, our debates over educational approaches and child rearing practices will change radically. The differences, for example, between "strict" and "permissive" parenting disappear when seen in the context of children's liberation because even the most permissive approaches then seem embarrassingly authoritarian. With respect to schools, making minor adjustments in present teaching methods becomes a meaningless exercise when we consider the prospect of children designing their own educational experiences. And the rhetoric about the psychological needs of children will have to be reevaluated to apply to children who will be free to choose their own ways of living rather than having to settle for what adults have unilaterally determined to be best for them.

When people first hear of children's liberation, they too often think of it in terms of parents who withdraw from their children, treat them in a laissez-faire manner, abandon any regulations or restrictions. Some even fear the reversal of conditions that now prevail, where children would dominate their parents, become demanding and intimidating. Neither concept is intended, and, of course, neither is desirable.

Granting children rights does not mean abandoning all concern for children, nor negating all that adults have to offer them. It does not mean giving up the possibility of living with them in an orderly and civilized manner. The exercise of adult judgment, wisdom, influence, and persuasion should be enhanced, not impaired. As always, children will become socialized and acculturated mainly through the imitation of adult models.

Children's liberation does not mean a negation of *all* standards, just *double* standards. Behavior will still be guided by ethics, morals, beliefs, and laws. Just as adults must abide by regulations, standards, and schedules, so children must responsibly abide by these same rules. No parent, for example, should feel any more compelled to cater to the capricious whims of a child, than he would to any adult member of the family. After all, the objective of any liberation effort is to reduce the many ways in which people victimize each other. Parents are already overly victimized and need liberation in their own right. The fundamental rule should be no victimization, in either direction.

Some people fear that granting full rights of citizenship to children might make them into little adults and cheat them out of their childhood. Actually, the result would be just the opposite. Liberation would help give children back their childhood. Children are now so dominated and programmed that they are indeed being robbed of childhood. The pressures to achieve scholastically and the restrictions on children's mobility combine to make a childhood full of pleasure, invention, and exploration much too foreign to today's child.

When it comes right down to it, we don't know much about what childhood should be or, for that matter, what it is actually like now. Many of our ideas are probably more myth than reality. We prize certain qualities of childhood, seeking them for ourselves—emotional honesty, lack of inhibition, clear perceptions, and moments of great joy and abandon. But on the other hand, childhood isn't all that its more romantic publicists would have us believe. We have the idea that if a person isn't holding a job he must be enjoying himself. So we think of childhood as carefree, when it is actually a difficult, worrisome time for most children. We think of it as a gentle time, when actually childhood can be violent, coarse, and cruel. We think of it as a time of unfolding, of great curiosity and excitement, when actually most children are bored. We think of it as a time of innocence, when actually children can be quite knowing and seductive.

As unsettling as the prospect of children's liberation may be, it is helpful to remember that demands for children's rights are not meant to destroy family life, but to improve it; not meant to end education, but to vitalize it; not meant to rupture the relationship of adult to child, but to enhance it; not meant to undermine parents, but to liberate them; not meant to threaten society's survival capability, but to strengthen it.

One would think that children's liberation would be a movement to which everyone could belong because everyone either is or has been a child. Unfortunately, that is true only in a limited sense. For most of us childhood is almost completely forgotten. We might just as well not have been children for all we can remember about it. We can all remember incidents from our childhood, sometimes even into the very early years, though rarely before the age of five or six. But what we remember is so fragmentary and so clouded by romantic myths of childhood that it is almost impossible to bring any intelligent conjecture based upon these memories to bear on the current problems of childhood.

If you think back into your own childhood, you will be able to recall only a handful of memories. Some you have heard about from others, some you have thought of before; all of them will be somewhat distorted, not only in the memory itself, but in the retelling. Even though it is possible to remember parts of one's childhood through intensive psychoanalysis, the reconstruction tends to follow the theories of the analyst who is guiding the process of remembering. For example, sexual fantasies about one's parents might be the most sought-after recollections. Memories relating to the politics of one's childhood, the oppression and impotence, may not be so systematically reassembled.

Memories are too often recalled only to reinforce some adult argument such as, "I always hated getting spanked, but I believe it was good for me," or "I never wanted to learn the piano, but I'm glad my parents made me practice," or "That teacher was the toughest one I had, but I certainly learned the most from her." The memory is distorted to fit the adult values.

A special kind of consciousness-raising is required to recall the boredom, the outrage, and the frustration of those years. We would much prefer to remember the cute things, the naughty things, the smart things, the behavior that will now gain us the appreciation of our adult peers, or which will capture the imagination of our youthful listeners. At a deeper level these romanticized and fragmentary memories of childhood only make trouble for today's children.

To say that this is everybody's revolution because we were all once children is not sufficient to justify adult participation in it. We are not children. Indeed, adults are for the most part the child's political enemy. Children should be making their own case. After all, the right to self-determination is one of the basic rights in children's liberation. But children are so oppressed and incapacitated that it is not at all likely that they will be able to act on their own behalf, at least not until they develop greater strength and vision as a group. Shulamith Firestone argues for feminist involvement in the struggle for children's rights because of women's long period of related sufferings with children and because, "There are no children yet able to write their own books, tell their own story. We will have to, one last time, do it for them."[2]

For a time then, there will be a role for adults who can take the position of advocates for children who cannot adequately represent themselves. Hopefully those adult efforts will give way eventually to the self-determined efforts of children themselves. Until then we will need more, not less, adult advocacy.

Child advocates now fall into two obviously related groups whose goals both overlap and conflict: on the one hand there are those who are interested in protecting children, and on the other those who are interested in protecting children's rights. The first, motivated by a concern for the basic helplessness of children, rely heavily on adult intervention in situations which victimize children, on their role as protectors, on their power to exercise their own authority in lieu of the child's. This group of advocates, by far the largest, is responsible for a remarkable amount of protective legislation for children and for making visible many of the ways in which children are abused and victimized. Advocates of this persuasion tend to take for granted the permanent disability of children and their lack of power to act for themselves. Unfortunately their efforts to "help little children" have led to paternalistic attitudes which may eventually have just the opposite effect.

The second group of advocates believes that ultimately children will be most helped not by continual intervention to protect them, but by work to secure their basic rights of citizenship. Believing strongly in the potential of children to act for themselves, their interests lean more toward liberation than protection. Their commitment to freedom for children is a strongly ideological one deriving historically from Rousseau through John Dewey and more recently Paul Goodman, Carl Rogers, A. S. Neill, and Wilhelm Reich.[3]

America has a long tradition of people helping oppressed groups to which they do not themselves belong, even when they themselves are regarded as oppressors. Whites were active in the emancipation of blacks. Men have been helpful in reducing the oppression of women. So it is that adults are working to help children.

The greatest resistance to the prospect of children's liberation will predictably come from those who are closest to the problem: parents, teachers, and children themselves. Parents respond, "My children are liberated enough"; "Children can't have it both ways, can't be equal to me and expect me to keep on working to support them"; "As far as I'm concerned children already have too much power." If that sounds familiar it is because one could substitute "women" or "wife" for "children" and have the very same responses made by husbands to the prospect of women's liberation. The early days of that movement were characterized by suggestions that women were already dominating, too powerful, and already in control of all the money and resources. Derision and ridicule always come from the groups where interdependence is greatest. Married men against women, Southern whites against blacks, and parents against children.

Paradoxical as it may seem, a good rule of thumb is to expect the greatest resistance from those who stand to benefit most. Just as blacks and women who have not had their consciousness raised are the greatest burdens of those movements, the Uncle

Toms and Aunt Toms, we can predict that children will be their own worst enemies in the movement for their liberation.

Perhaps no single group of people has been studied more than children, both scientifically and clinically. A large body of literature on children and childhood has developed and a complete and separate discipline has emerged. Research has given us a more comprehensive understanding of the thought processes, attitudes, behavior, developmental stages, and interpersonal dynamics of children than we have of any other class of people.

Recognizing the politics of childhood, however, may force us back into the laboratory and clinic to reevaluate our research on children for the simple reason that research done on any group of people in an atmosphere of prejudice and subjugation is bound to be full of systematic error. Just as we have had to rethink the early research on blacks before we started calling them blacks, and women before we started to question that they might not be fulfilled in a subordinate role to men, it will now be necessary to question our findings about children.

Elaine Simpson, a child researcher at the University of California at Berkeley, questions our scientific understanding of children:

> If I were able to drop some old assumptions and projections, what might I see differently in the play of these preschoolers I have been

> observing? Of course I have no way of knowing. The problem is that we must clarify, not only child psychology or primitive mentality, but our own and we must be ready to discover the common ground of humanity between ourselves and young children. We must be willing to subjectively entertain the possibility that childish behavior is no different from our own behavior faced with a similar degree of unknowns and handicaps. It is certainly easier to think of children as inferior adults or potential adults or as an entirely different manner of creature altogether from ourselves, easier to argue whether they need to be treated strictly or with indulgence, easier to investigate ways in which their thinking follows a different logic than our own, easier to think of them happily engaged in wishful thinking and the pursuit of immediate gratifications and unable to cope with the important problems of life with which we cope. As long as the emphasis is on the differences which exist or can be made to appear to exist between ourselves and our child subjects, we run the danger of remaining blind to some common ground of humanity and to our own intuition and empathy which may be needed for meaningful and important interpretations of child behavior.[4]

To the question of what we really know about the potentialities of children, the answer will have to be that we do not know what children can do when they are at their best because we have not created the conditions necessary to elicit superior behavior. Indeed, in our society, it is virtually impossible to create such conditions. Until we develop a new appreciation for their rights and a new respect for their potential, we cannot know children.

In addition to the thousands of studies of children, there are hundreds of books giving advice on how to raise children. While many of the suggestions provided are fascinating, the overwhelming problem with all of these books is that they convey the erroneous idea that it is indeed possible to raise children; that there is a way to do it; that one can successfully manage, control, stimulate, and motivate them; that one can make them creative, well-mannered, healthy, adjusted, informed, and aspiring; and that one can discharge these responsibilities with judgment, taste, style, contentment, intelligence, and a minimum of frustration and doubt.

What the books don't tell is that being a good parent isn't just difficult, it's impossible. There is simply no way to be a good parent in a society organized against children. The best things that happen between parent and child happen by accident or by surprise, very often breaking all rules. Anyone who isn't bewildered by child rearing and doesn't find it an extremely formidable and trying experience, probably isn't a parent.

Parenting, as philosopher Abraham Kaplan points out, is not a problem but a dilemma. Problems are solvable; dilemmas are not. Nor should they be. Rearing a child is like having a romance; it is not a set of problems to be solved but a relationship to be experienced. Most of the important relationships in our lives are like that. Marriage surely is. Dilemmas must be lived.

We probably would not want to "manage" such relationships anyway. A managed relationship differs from an experienced one the way a seduction differs from a romance. It is more important for us to be vulnerable to relationships. Vulnerability, after all, is really the only thing we have to give. Probably that is what it means to give oneself.

We have the idea as we read these books on child rearing that we learn from our own failures and other people's successes. It is probably just the reverse: we learn from our own successes and others' failures. Perhaps the best kind of book that could be written would be a book discussing the failures of the people whom we always believed were the most expert.

When it comes to human relationships, no one has a corner on the market of knowledge. The most eminent people in the field have their share of doubts and insecurities. To believe that those who write about child rearing are the personification of their books is to be greatly misled. Rather than being disappointed by this, we should be tremendously reassured by it. We are all in this together. If anything, people should be made to feel less guilty and pressured, less afraid that they are going about their lives incorrectly, less needful of comparing themselves to others. Everyone needs liberation from that kind of oppression.

Parents need to be freed from the burden of guilt that comes from believing that they are solely responsible for what their children become. Most of what happens to children, even what parents do to their own children, is well beyond the parents' control. We carry too much guilt over being strict or indulgent, being away from our children or around them, being up on the latest theories or ignorant of them, when actually none of this matters much in determining whether or not our children grow up to be good people. Even that most guilt-producing factor of all, the "broken family," makes little if any difference in shaping our children's lives toward good or evil. In a liberated society, parents would not need to feel guilty about their failure to make a success of the nuclear family, or about not being all-wise in matters of child rearing, or in sometimes not setting a good example, or any of a million ordinary frailties or inevitable social conditions that now produce an abundance of unnecessary guilt.

Clinical psychologist Bernard Apfelbaum describes the benefit to adults of these new ways of viewing the parent-child relationship:

> What a relief children's liberation would be to parents—to learn that the responsibilities they are so ill-suited and ill-trained for turn out to be largely unnecessary; to discover that child

> training is impossible, illusory and an incubus upon the parents, demeaning and dehumanizing both parent and child. Surely child abuse must be caused at least partly by the inability to protect oneself against those one feels responsible for but feels impotent to help.
> We need children as friends and intimates, as minds and reflections. Parents need to identify with their children as much as children need to identify with their parents. But these processes are interfered with as long as children are niggers. Children's liberation is truly parent liberation.[5]

There is no way to have a liberated society until we have liberated children. But people are not liberated one by one. They must be liberated as a class. To do that we must examine the ways that we, as a society, discriminate against children—the ways that make their lives, and consequently ours, so limited and difficult.

2

The Invention of Children

Children did not always exist; they were invented. The idea of childhood is a European invention of the sixteenth century. Before the latter part of the Middle Ages there simply was no concept of childhood. Most languages had no words meaning child. [1]

Today we look at these little people around us and think that we know what they are. But what they are is actually what we have come to think about them. They are our invention. The concept of childhood has changed so radically throughout history and from culture to culture that there is no way of establishing historically or culturally what a child is; no fixed concept of childhood, but rather a concept highly vulnerable to change. Undoubtedly, it will soon change again in response to the rapid shifts in human affairs which characterize the twentieth century.

We have named these little people "children" and we have come to regard them as special. But childhood is not a natural state. It is a myth. The myth of childhood constantly changes in response to other developments in civilization. This we know mainly through the scholarship of historian Philippe Aries. His *Centuries of Childhood* is the major source of information about the incredible development of the idea of childhood. [2]

In medieval times and before, childhood was simply of no importance. No records were kept of childbirth or age; a child of "about seven" could be any age between five and nine. No children appear in art until the twelfth century. Even then, they are portrayed as little adults, they display the physical proportions and musculature of adults, and wear the adult clothing.[3] In every respect they are miniature adults. The differences between the shapes of children and the shapes of adults were not recognized throughout the ancient civilizations until the Renaissance. The notable exception is in Greek art of the Hellenistic period in which the child's physical proportions (but not the child as part of the social structure) were realistically portrayed in the shape of little Eroses, mythical creatures with rounded bodies. After the Hellenistic period, these children disappeared from iconography for many centuries.

In the thirteenth century the child first began to appear in art. No one knows why children did not seem to be of any importance prior to that time. Perhaps it was because most children died. Until very recent times a great many children died in their early years, most at childbirth or during the first year of infancy. One had to have many children to keep a few. Montaigne was reported to have said casually, "All mine die," as if he were a gardener talking about his cabbages.[4] People did not attach much importance to children, perhaps because of the great chance of losing them. But this interpretation, of course, reflects our twentieth-century attitudes about how parents value their children.

Childhood became important as a result of the profound changes in our civilization surrounding the Reformation and Renaissance. It was not the new humanists but the new moralists, mainly Jesuits, who came to see children as "fragile creatures of God who need to be both safeguarded and reformed." With the advent of this attitude children came to be valued as potential adults. Now they were to need education and protection. Childhood became preparation for adulthood. Before this period children just grew up; after this period they had to be raised. Before that time they were inconsequential, undefined little people; after that time they became "children," meaning adults-in-training.

As childhood became more important, society for the first time began associating it with all sorts of negative qualities: irrationality, imbecility, weakness, prelogicism, and primitivism.[5] It is difficult for our present culture to appreciate that these demeaning views of children are a recent development, appearing only after childhood acquired increased significance. And with this new importance, came, for the first time, antipathy toward the child, the beginnings of our present resentment.

Before the seventeenth century, children were not thought of as innocent. Only then did innocence become the idea of childhood. It was at that time that children were no longer given indecent books to read and life began to be hidden from them. Previously, adults in the presence of children had talked and acted openly about sex and every other "adult" matter. There was considerable sexual precocity. Louis XIV was in his wife's bed at age fourteen. Girls often married at thirteen. It was common for an adult to play with a child's genitals (this is still practiced in Moslem countries). But in the seventeenth century children began to be seen as requiring protection and were separated from information about the private lives of adults. In medieval times children were unimportant but enjoyed, even coddled; from the seventeenth century on, children needed to be reformed. Today's parents and children still carry the grim burdens of that major historical change.

The potentialities of children seem to be limited only by cultural expectations. In other cultures children are betrothed at birth and married at nine or ten; they become warriors and hunters as early as eight in the Sioux tribes; they give birth at the earliest possible ages, and go through the rites of passage at ten or twelve in some Nigerian villages.

It is not uncommon in some cultures to see children of two or three actually spending a great deal of time fulfilling the responsibility of caring for younger children, or helping with daily chores.

Among the Gusii of Kenya, the child is considered capable of training at two and is forced into obedience and the assumption of near-adult responsibilities by the age of six or seven. Young Cheyenne Indian boys are given little bows and arrows as soon as they can walk.

In pre-revolutionary Mexico peasant boys of six or seven were likely to be put to work looking after the oxen and carrying water. Among the Hausa of Nigeria, young girls of eight or nine are expected to carry food and water to the men in the fields. From the age of nine or ten Klamath Indian girls learn to gather and grind their staple diet, and to make mats, baskets, and clothing.[6]

As soon as they can toddle, the children of the East African Chaga are at work looking after smaller babies, carrying water or firewood, helping to prepare food, cleaning animal quarters, sweeping the yard, cutting fodder, and thatching the house.

But the American culture has developed a myth of childhood in which children are special creatures who must be handled in a special way. Anthropologist Mary Ellen Goodman says, "We have set a new record; no other people seems ever to have been so preoccupied with children, so anxious about them, or so uncertain of how to deal with them."[7]

Our society is now segregated not only by race, class and sex, but by age. Consequently ideas about childhood are being developed and reinforced not through contact between adults and children, but through the lack of it. There was no age separation before the sixteenth century, no separate world for children. They were in on everything, they shared everything, the same games, stories, dances, toys. Adults and children were never apart. All paintings of the time which showed groups of people, showed—without exception—children in the company of adults, playing, nursing, or urinating—a fully accepted part of life.

Boarding schools, which developed in the seventeenth century, were the beginning of age segregation. Since then, children and adults have gradually separated so that now the segregation is almost complete.

Children were not grouped by age in school until the nineteenth century. Previously, schools resembled what we now call open classrooms. All students did a variety of things. Older and younger children worked and learned together. The teacher did not supervise the activities closely but might be found working or talking with a small cluster of children. This format existed not because a sophisticated pedagogy was being followed, but because at the time children's age differences just weren't very important to society. Carefully working along with the child's development through progressive stages of growth was unheard of. Ages did not matter much.[8]

The fairly recent idea of paying attention to children should not be confused with affection for children. It is, as a matter of fact, just the opposite. With importance and attention came resentment. It became important to shape children, to reform them, to fix them, to correct them, to discipline them, to educate them, until we have now become obsessed with physical, moral, and sexual problems of children.

The responsibility for reforming the child was first the school's. Only later did the family become an agency to accomplish the task of molding children's bodies and souls.

But the family, as we know it, is also a fairly recent invention. It was not always the sentimental unit it now is. It's main function throughout most of history was to pass along name and property. It wasn't until the sixteenth and seventeenth centuries that the family based on affectional bonds rose in importance. Before that time the family simply didn't have a sentimental existence, especially among the poor. Children were valued for their contribution to the common good. They were regularly apprenticed out at the age of eight to work as bonded servants in other households, where they would live for a period of seven to nine years.

The nuclear family (two adults and their minor children) is very recent—a twentieth-century development. It is a completely self-contained unit, not requiring help from others, not dependent upon the community. The parents have responsibility for the total care of the children, care which once was distributed among several adults in an extended family. The children do little for the family and almost nothing for each other or for themselves. Already-overburdened parents continue to increase their sense of responsibility and their feeling of guilt over these responsibilities as society's expectations of what families should offer their children rise. Nevertheless, the popularity of the nuclear family as the ideal continues in spite of the accelerating difficulties.

Before the advent of the nuclear family, parents could rely on the whole community in which they lived to help rear their children. But now the situation has become so particularized that adults will not let others touch their children. We fear that there is something perverse or meddling about those in our community who do. In contrast to this, other cultures depend upon communal care and as a consequence parents are relieved of the responsibility for constant supervision and attention that must ordinarily be given to children.

Not the least of the changes which make childhood so different today has to do with the changing balance of education and information for adults and children, a balance shifting now to children. For the first time in history, we may be experiencing a reversal in the transmission of culture, with the young teaching the old. Now, for the first time, youth is truly on the leading edge of our society. Although they are less experienced, they are better educated and even better informed. Older people still have a great deal to teach young people, but the amount that young people can now teach adults is greater than ever.

One of the most serious consequences of our limited view of children and of our segregation of them is that we may be subverting their capacity for genius. It has been pointed out that we no longer have infant and child prodigies, or that at least they are now much rarer than before.[9] In medieval times when children were an integral part of the community, they did show great genius. Louis XIII performed all sorts of remarkable feats by the age of two. He played the violin at seventeen months and played tennis when he still slept in a cradle. He was an archer and played cards and chess at six. Today we might worry a bit about precocity of that magnitude. Then, people took it for granted. They accepted it as a gift that anyone might have, but didn't associate the remarkable achievements with age.

Child prodigies began to disappear in the eighteenth century. We sacrificed genius for our present interest in homogeneity. We began to dislike precocity in children and to dislike children themselves. Our insistence on uniformity began the modern oppression of children.

3

Self-determination and the Double Standard

Children are treated as the private property of their parents. Technically the law no longer regards children as chattel, but in practice the child does indeed still belong to his parent. The parent has both the right and responsibility to control the life of the child.

Children have come to be like adult toys. Consumer items. "Should we buy a new car this year, or have a baby?" And well parents might conjecture, because children are no longer a financial asset, but a distinct financial liability. Now that they can no longer help on the farm or in the factory, the only way children feel they can serve is by giving parents affection and gratitude, and by meeting their parents' expectations for them. This condition, although it does not require drudgery and slavery, in other respects differs little from the ancient relationships of the parent to the child in that the parent dominates and the child serves, leaving little room for the self-determined choice of the child.

Children, like adults, should have the right to decide the matters which affect them most directly. The issue of self-determination is at the heart of children's liberation. It is, in fact, the only issue, a definition of the entire concept. The acceptance of the child's right to self-determination is fundamental to all the rights to which children are entitled.

It is especially difficult to accept the idea of self-determination when it comes to decisions close to home. Children would, for example, have the right to exercise self-determination in decisions about eating, sleeping, playing, listening, reading, washing, and dressing. They would have the right to choose their associates, the opportunity to decide what life goals they wish to pursue, and the freedom to engage in whatever activities are permissible for adults.

The right to self-determination is the right to a single standard of morals and behavior for children and adults. No more double standard. What's good for the goose is good for the gosling. Children would have the right to engage in acts which are now acceptable for adults but not for children, and they would not be required to gain permission to do something if such permission is automatically granted to adults.

The term "self-determination" is inevitably connected with the concept of freedom. This connection makes the issue difficult to deal with objectively because the word "freedom" is loaded with emotion, has so many different connotations, and is invested with deep philosophical meanings. There is freedom as opposed to communism, freedom and democracy, freedom versus determinism; the paradox that one is most free when most constrained, that expanding choices limits freedom; freedom from as different from freedom to; freedom of the spirit, freedom of behavior; freedom, liberty and license—the list is endless.

The argument as to whether or not one can ever be truly free and self-determining has occupied philosophers, theologians, and psychologists for centuries. For example, the followers of the behaviorist school of psychology led presently by B. F. Skinner hold that freedom is a fiction, that behavior is controlled and determined by environmental forces and developmental conditioning, and that freedom and self-determination are, by definition, not possible for anyone.[1]

But to the extent that the terms freedom and self-determination have meaning for adults, and to the extent that adults have a right to self-determination, children should have that same right. The freedom associated with children's liberation means essentially the freedom that adults enjoy.

Of course freedom is not license. Freedom for a child does not mean the right to limit other people's right to freedom. A. S. Neill of *Summerhill* suggests this definition: "I define license as interfering with another's freedom. For example in my school a child is free to go to lessons or to stay away from lessons because that is his own affair, but he is not free to play a trumpet when others want to study or sleep." [2]

Some parents whose basic approach to their children already minimizes the power relationship between adult and child will have less difficulty in squaring these ideas with their own concepts of freedom and responsible child rearing. But for most parents, and for that matter most children, these ideas will seem foreign indeed. They will argue that the right to self-determination will bring with it the risk of physical and psychological damage. No doubt some risks are involved. But risks compared to what?

Under present conditions in our society many children are severely and constantly damaged —physically, socially, and emotionally. And all children are to some degree limited and incapacitated by our institutions and by systematic discrimination against them. Compared to what exists now, the risks of harming children by accepting their right to self-determination may be greatly overrated.

It's time to admit that no one knows how to grow people. The situation is truly paradoxical. Many of our most valuable people have come from the most calamitous early childhood situations. Investigations of the childhoods of eminent people expose the fact that they did not receive anything like the kind of child rearing that a person in our culture is led to believe is healthy for children.[3] Many were abused, rejected, disciplined, dominated, ignored, disliked, brutalized, treated with contempt, left on their own; their parents were demanding, alcoholic, cruel, bizarre, insane. Of course there were parents who were devoted, coddling and affectionate as well. Apparently the only factor that was relatively constant was that the parents frequently held high expectations for themselves and their children. Whether in spite of or because of these conditions, it is clear that these children not only survived, but reached great heights of achievement, many after having experienced the most deplorable and traumatic childhoods.

Not only do people survive calamity, they often mature as a result of it. One can even make a good case for a calamity theory of growth. Very often it is the crisis situation, the serious injury, illness, or accident, the loss of a loved one, the going through a divorce, the birth of a retarded or crippled child, or the learning that one has a terminal disease that actually improves us as human beings. Paradoxically, while these incidents can sometimes ruin people, they are usually growth experiences. As a result of such calamities the person often makes a major reassessment of his life situation and changes it in ways that reflect a deeper understanding of his own capabilities, values, and goals. There are also happy calamities such as inheriting money, having a baby, or becoming president of a large company which also tend to change people, often for the better.

It may be that the situations we try hardest to avoid, for ourselves and for our children, would actually be the most beneficial to us. Yet we obviously can't design such calamities for a child to experience just because it might be good for him. We might, however, be able to take a more relaxed look at the possible dangers involved in the child's right to self-determination. The fact is that we know very little about the necessary ingredients to make a good human being. There simply are no experts in this field.

In another sense, asking what is good for children is beside the point. We will grant children rights for the same reason we grant rights to adults, not because we are sure that children will then become better people, but more for ideological reasons, because we believe that expanding freedom as a way of life is worthwhile in itself. And freedom, we have found, is a difficult burden for adults as well as children.

The achievement of children's rights must apply to children of all ages, from birth to adulthood. Some of the rights may seem inappropriate to apply to the very young because of the obvious incapacities of small children. But rights cannot be withheld from the very young solely on the basis of age any more than they can be withheld from the very old who may be similarly incapacitated. The inability to exercise one's rights at any age, old or young, should simply mean that even greater care must be taken by society to guarantee the protection of these rights.

The idea of children living under the same rules as adults raises all sorts of fears and anxieties in those of us who have come to believe that it is our job to control and protect children. These concerns are the barriers to the achievement of self-determination in children and must be faced directly, for self-determination as a principle is fundamental to any discussion of specific rights for children. It is the cornerstone upon which the others are built.

The fundamental barrier, of course, is our deeply-held belief in the innocence and helplessness of children. This belief is probably more the product of a seventeenth-century mentality than it is of a careful assessment of the capabilities and potentialities of children today. Moreover, as long as we deprive the child of his right to self-determination we cannot even assess his potentialities. While it is certain that society actually creates innocence and helplessness in children, we do not, and cannot, know if there are in fact any characteristics that are inherent in children. The jury is still out.

Rather than debating that issue, a more valuable and pertinent task might be to evaluate the consequences and risks involved in granting children the right to self-determination. The reasons most adults don't permit children to be self-determining have more to do with what they perceive to be dangers and discomforts rather than any desire to limit children unnecessarily. These reasons stem mainly from expediency, habit, and tradition. Since most concerns are likely to center primarily on the problems and possibilities of actually having to live with a self-determining child, perhaps the most pertinent analysis to be made is of the child's behavior in the home.

One would think that if self-determination and children's liberation were to exist anywhere they should exist in the home. Surely, one might think, "If I can't liberate my *own* child in my *own* home, then how can children's liberation ever come about in society at large?" Actually it may be that the home only *seems* to be a likely place to start. It is traditional to think that way (for example, "charity begins at home"), but usually it is the *most* difficult place to make changes, not the least difficult. For parents to feel frustrated or guilty about their failures in liberating their own children is groundless.

Liberation does not begin at home. Granting children the right to self-determination in the home, with respect to sleeping, eating, or dressing only *looks* as if it should be easy. To the contrary, it is virtually impossible. For a number of reasons. The main one is that the home is not separate from the rest of society. People cannot be liberated in the home, which seems to be an isolated circumstance but is actually a part of the larger system, as long as the major forces of society continue to oppress. We do not shed our culture when we enter our homes. Parents cannot help but feel a responsibility to do things much as others in the community would have them done. The parent who feels he cannot liberate his child because he fails to do so at home does not understand the pervasive and complex political problems involved in children's liberation. It cannot be done at home because it has not been done in society.

Nevertheless, discussing the child's behavior in the home can be valuable for several reasons. First, although the decisions to be considered may seem of minor importance, the parent can gain some insight into the process of self-determination for his children, and the child can begin to consider new ways of making judgments and solving problems. Second, it helps one to recognize the sources of concern and to evaluate the risks in self-determination. Third, it illustrates in microcosm, and perhaps more graphically, the dimensions of the problem as it might exist in society at large. Fourth, it confronts the fact that the home situation is indeed connected to, and to a large degree determined by, forces well beyond the control of any parent.

Take the problem of self-determination with respect to a child's eating. No one, for example, should be expected to prepare a meal at a special time for a child simply because he chooses not to eat at the regular dinner hour. Most children could, with some special arrangements and training, prepare meals for themselves if necessary. Those children whose schedules demand special timetables would receive the same consideration afforded any adult member of the household in similar circumstances. But the manageable concerns end here.

It is not reassuring to the parent who is worried that his child get the right things to eat to be told that infants naturally choose a balanced diet and will not eat what they don't want anyway, or that children usually eat more, not less, than they need. Part of the reason that the parent cannot relax about this problem is that the general situation in which the child finds himself works against a healthy solution. The unbalanced diets of middle-class children result as much as anything from the fact that soft drinks, candy, chewing gum, potato chips, cereal, snacks, and quick-service hot dogs and hamburgers are far more likely to be advertised to children than fruit, vegetables, meat, fish, eggs, and other foods most people consider healthy. The problem is largely one of consumer exploitation. If children could gain control over such exploitation, then parents might be less concerned about controlling their eating habits.

Loss of authority to control a child does not mean that the child cannot be influenced. In the absence of authoritarian control, adult judgment and information is more likely to be offered and accepted. Good nutrition is no doubt important for children (and adults) to learn, but one learns them best by example and informed conversation.

To take another problem, most parents know that children enjoy sleeping as well as adults and that their resistance to it comes partly because they know it is a good way to get their parents' attention and partly because they know that many interesting "adult" activities take place after their bedtime. But the sleeping habits of both adults and children are governed largely by the pressures to engage in productive activity during the daytime hours. We adhere to nighttime sleeping hours because it is convenient for our work schedules. For most children it is necessary to follow daytime hours to fulfill their compulsory attendance in school—and the parent can go to jail if he doesn't see that the child attends school regularly. If these restrictions did not exist, children would, of course, have more latitude in the choice of sleeping hours.

An example of current bedtime practice is offered by child specialist Haim Ginott who suggests that the child should not have a fixed bedtime but that a range of time, say between the hours of 8 and 10, be set by parents with the child selecting a particular hour to go to bed within that time period.[4] While this moves in the direction of placing more control in the hands of the child, in its fundamental philosophy the control stays with the parents and the need for coercion and threat remains necessary. Moreover, some parents find that given these limits, the child will regularly choose the upper limit. The maintenance of adult authority in this case might actually have made the bedtime hour later than it would have been if the child were entirely self-determining in the matter.

If children made these decisions for themselves—and suffered the consequences—they would be capable in the long run of learning, as most adults have, that when one is too tired his day is less enjoyable. They might discover, a bit earlier than usual perhaps, that there is some wisdom in their parent's advice. At least it would make the ritual of going to bed less of a vehicle through which parents and children express their mutual antagonisms. Believe it or not, however, for some parents this is not a big issue. Their children either go to bed by themselves or they are simply covered up on the spot where they drop off to sleep.

What about other physical dangers? The child running or playing where he might be hit or injure himself? The first answer is that, of course, we cannot risk a child's death. Just as we would pull an adult out of the path of an onrushing car, we would do the same for a child. There is no double standard in the emergency situation. The problem of having to constantly control and supervise our children only arises because of the potential dangers of playing in or near the streets. We are forced into this posture because our traffic systems have not been designed with child safety as a high priority. Instead, designers have placed the responsibility to protect the child with the parent, and the parent has accepted it without even realizing that there might be another way. Obviously our need to control children and to prohibit them from being self-determining decreases as our attention to better design increases.

Life is inevitably risky and almost everyone agrees that it is important that the child be given the opportunity to take risks in order to develop as a whole person, to push his limits, to discover his potentialities. Children may ride horses, dive from high places, play football, and engage in all sorts of strenuous and even dangerous athletics. Most sports involve some physical risks, and the elimination of all danger in our society is certainly not a realistic or desirable goal. If we could solve the one problem of the automobile, we will have come a long way in making the world safer for children and enabling them to become more self-determining.

In each of these instances—eating, sleeping, and avoiding physical danger—there is the built-in learning factor of behavior having its own reward and punishment. Proper eating is rewarded with good digestion and a sense of well-being, eventually if not immediately; improper eating is similarly punished, ultimately if not immediately. The same is true for getting enough sleep: when one doesn't have enough, his schedule must change to accommodate the deficiency. With respect to physical dangers of an accidental sort, the risks one takes in pushing the limits are felt immediately when the risk has been too great. To make it possible for children to be self-determining, however, we must find ways of eliminating lethal dangers, where the first lesson is the last one.

It is understandable that parents feel justified in resorting to authoritative measures of control in order to protect their child's health. One only needs to have dealt with a sick or injured child to realize how painful that experience is, not only for the child but for the adult who feels responsible. No wonder parents feel that they must make their children do the things that will be good for them. On the other hand, the same is true with respect to children's attitudes toward adults. Children want their parents to be healthy and happy. For obvious reasons nothing could be much more important to them. They don't want them to do things that will make them irritable or sick or endanger their lives. Children are continually trying to keep their parents from chain-smoking, drinking too much, getting too fat, driving dangerously, staying up too late, going out too often, or working too hard. But the child has no control over the parent in this regard. Just because the child is right and wise in these matters, should he have the power to force his parents to take better care of themselves, even if it's for their own good?

The liberation of the individual child is virtually impossible because most decisions and actions are simply not up to the parent or the child, but require a change in society, a social support system. To take one small example, consider the situation of the child who chooses his own clothes. The parent understandably dreads taking the child to nursery school with dirty or mismatched clothes, for he must parade his child in front of critical parents who are competing to have the most attractive child in the class. As long as that competition persists, the pressures on the parent are almost insurmountable. If, however, the group of parents from that school were to get together to discuss the ways in which their attitudes toward the problem force such restrictions on the child, they might be able to establish a new set of ground rules, ones that would be liberating to both the child and to themselves. The parents might be able to agree, as a group, that they would no longer determine the dress of the child by any arbitrary, coercive, or domineering methods. This would mean that they would have to accept any mismatched outfits, not as evidence of parental neglect or ineptitude, but as evidence that they are now observing a new set of ground rules. In this way, what might have been a minus turns into a plus. It is far from easy to accomplish these arrangements because we are not good at developing such social support systems. But it does illustrate in a microcosm what might happen on a larger scale if we were able to adopt a new set of expectations about childhood and parenting.

The concept most difficult for parents to accept is that they will have responsibility without authority. It is basic to most philosophies of parenthood that one's authority must equal one's responsibility.

We seldom realize that they have never matched. No one has ever had enough authority to deal adequately with responsibilities—especially parents.

With the advent of children's rights the parent will not have authoritarian control upon which to rely. He will have to depend more heavily on judgment, advice, and persuasion. But it is also crucial to recognize that the responsibilities which parents now have will diminish and change. The problem is that we always lose authority long before we lose responsibility.

4

The Right to Alternative Home Environments

People who are asked to explain their success often reply with the timeworn remark, "The most important thing I did was to choose my parents very carefully." The statement underscores how important our parents are to whatever we become as adults—how hopelessly dependent we are on their genes, their values, and their child rearing practices—and how impossible it is to do anything about it.

As parents now perceive the situation, it is their fundamental right to have children and to raise them as they see fit. The 1970 White House Conference on Children, however, offered a different view. The conference held that the rights of parents cannot infringe upon the rights of children.[1] As a society we may soon come to a similar conclusion, that the ability to conceive a child gives one no right to raise that child, and that raising a child gives one no right to dominate or to abuse him. The decisions about a child's home environment should not belong to his parents alone. The child must have some right to choose also. And if he is too young to choose, his rights must be protected by having an advocate acting in his behalf.

Although the child cannot choose his parents in the genetic sense, he should be able to choose them in an environmental sense. The child cannot avoid deriving his genetic makeup from his parents, but he should have the opportunity, if he chooses, to avoid their daily influence. He must be provided with alternatives to his parents' home environment.

In spite of our romantic myths about natural families, parents are not all that necessary or beneficial for children. Parents understandably like to believe otherwise. Surely there are moments when parents feel especially qualified to be parents. And some parents seem remarkably capable of working special magic with their children. But this quality is by no means limited to the people who conceived the child.

Children need parents for the same reason that parents need children, simply because they have them. Once they have them they come to love and need them. The bonds are affectional rather than functional. There was a time when everyone in the family needed everyone else to fulfill some purposeful role: husbands needed wives to cook and sew, and wives needed husbands to provide and protect. Parents needed children to aid in the work, and children needed parents to shelter, feed, and clothe them. Each family member served highly functional roles: spinning yarn, fighting enemies, raising crops. We no longer have the survival and security needs of the frontier family. The services that our family members can provide are easily available in the nearby community. The frontier family came together for security and survival. In the process, the people who needed each other often came to love each other. Now the reverse is true: we need each other because we have come to love each other.

Our ideas about what children need are so colored by our myths of childhood, by our lack of respect for them, and by our devotion to the nuclear family that we can actually say very little about their "basic" needs. We do know that child-rearing practices differ widely from culture to culture. In some cultures the mother squats in the surf to deliver her baby, in some the newborn is placed in bed with the father; some children are wrapped tightly, some are always naked; some are allowed to wander around the community at will, some are kept virtually imprisoned in dark huts and are neither spoken to or played with for their first year; some have close ties with their father, some do not know their father; some are exposed to the elements as a test of maturity; some are held and fondled almost constantly; some are punished with severe physical violence, some are rarely punished. It is presumptuous to suggest that there is a way to raise children based upon their needs.

Although we must always question scientific evidence on children that has been developed in a culture which oppresses them, it nevertheless does appear that there are some generally accepted views of basic needs: children need loving care as newborns and in early infancy. They need, for what we would call normal physical growth, certain nutritive elements. For their minds to develop they need stimulation and variation. And as children grow older they need to be with adults with whom they can identify. Even with these so-called basics, there are disagreements and exceptions. But even if there weren't, there is nothing in these findings that would require any particular kind of home environment for the child at any age. Certainly there is no justification here for the nuclear family as the only model of family life.

Parenting in the nuclear family is so difficult, demanding, restricting, and expensive, and having children is so unbelievably burdensome that many couples, when they discover that they have conceived a child, really wish they hadn't. Most abortions are given to married mothers who *know* they don't want another child. A large percentage of all children conceived are not wanted. Once a child is born the parents often come to love the new baby, but still there is a possibility that it will remain to some extent unwanted and the target of the parents' resentment. This may help to account for the fact that so many children grow up in unhappy circumstances. Of course, it is not just unwanted children whose lives are miserable. Psychoanalyst James Thickstun flatly says that "in some respects at least everyone has had a wretched childhood."

The situation is worse than wretched for some children. We often forget that the most heinous crimes against children are committed by their natural parents. Until quite recently parental abuse of children has been a rather well-kept secret, kept by the child, by the parents, and unfortunately by the physicians who have given abused children medical attention. The facts were probably too horrifying to report, perhaps even to believe. But the X-ray evidence began to mount, overwhelming evidence that babies and children were coming back repeatedly to hospitals with dozens of different fractures, all supposedly caused accidentally. The medical profession finally recognized that parents do brutally mistreat their children and that such treatment is a major cause of infant death and trauma. Gradually within the medical profession there came to be a new responsibility and new ethical concern for more accurate reporting of the "battered child syndrome." [2]

Although it is likely that a great many incidents of parental brutality are still not reported, the numbers of children involved are overwhelming. Child abuse is one of the leading causes of child death. Although estimates vary, it can be conservatively stated that in the United States between sixty thousand and two hundred fifty thousand children are battered, burned, or starved by their parents each year, and some researchers estimate that the number may be as high as three or four million.[3] Several children die each day from such abuse; more die at the hands of their parents than from any single disease.[4]

Children are tied, gagged, whipped, systematically exposed to electric shock, made to swallow all kinds of noxious materials such as pepper, dirt, feces, urine, vinegar, alcohol; their skulls and bones have been broken—sometimes repeatedly—their faces and bodies lacerated, their eyes pounded, even gouged out. Children have had their arms cut off; they've been burned with lighted cigarettes, matches, steam pipes, hot irons; beaten with belts and baseball bats, held in ice water, had scalding water poured over their genitals, placed in roadways where autos would run over them, cooked in ovens, thrown off cliffs; they've been bitten, stabbed, shot, drowned, and smothered. The crimes of parents against their children are almost inconceivable.

Studies of child abuse in England by Eustace Chesser showed that between 6 and 7 percent of all children are "so neglected or ill-treated or become so maladjusted" as to come to the attention of the National Society for the Prevention of Cruelty to Children.[5] And this study was conducted *before* the battered child syndrome became recognized.

One fact is evident: while the natural parents of the child do not necessarily make the best parents, it is abundantly clear that they make the worst ones.

These parents who attack and torture and murder their children are from all classes, all races, all religions, all socioeconomic levels. Only one common feature seems to link most of them: parents who batter their children were often themselves battered as children. One cannot help but have sympathy for them. Not only did they have difficult times as children themselves but they usually love their children, and their children love them. It is a sad paradox that the severely unstable homes are the ones to which the child clings most tenaciously. It is, therefore, not easy to solve the problem by trying to remove the child from the home, for an absence of affection is not usually the primary issue.

In making the case for the need to have better home environments for children it is, of course, necessary to discuss these horrifying and all too frequent atrocities. But there is a danger in citing only the problems of the most tragically oppressed. The danger is that those parents who do not physically mutilate their children will compare themselves with the battering parents and come to feel that they themselves are different, humane, unoppressive. In the process of telling the most horrifying stories, the plight of the average child will be ignored. It is not just the battered children who grow up in oppressive circumstances, but all children. The kinds of oppression vary, but one kind is universal: the child has no alternative but to live with his parents or go to jail. Even if family life were delightful, and it often is, the child should have other options.

Although our image of the family is the nuclear family (usually pictured in advertising and on magazine covers with the husband slightly larger and older than the wife and the son slightly larger and older than the daughter), it is not actually the way most Americans live. About 60 percent live in some domestic arrangement other than the nuclear family: single people, married people without children, children living with stepparents, couples with grown children, single mothers, single fathers, elderly people living in nursing homes, convicts in prisons, students in residence halls, homosexual arrangements, etc. So while our whole society is structured around the nuclear family, most people don't live that way.

Nationally, three or four out of ten marriages end in divorce, and the rate is twice as high on the West Coast and in large urban centers. One might ask, "Is the concept of the American family really working? Is it a suitable place to raise children?" If we counter, "Compared to what?" we must answer "Yes" to both questions. Compared to what family life had been in the past there is little doubt that the present-day American family is better in almost every respect. It does have burdens the extended family did not have, but there were tremendous burdens of drudgery and patriarchy then. We tend to forget that the good old days never were. The question of whether the present family arrangement is a good place for children is an easy question to answer. It seems to be the *only* place for children. There are now no alternatives.

This problem shows up most clearly in our attempts to deal with runaways. Running away from home is serious business for five hundred thousand children each year who feel a real need to escape from their parents. Runaways are almost always returned to their homes by authorities, not just because they are regarded as the private property of adults, but because there is no place else for them to go, except to some sort of jail. We now treat children who leave their parents' house as law-breakers. The only recourse for a child who hates his situation is to ask the courts to intervene and determine the home an unsuitable place for him to be reared. Although the child usually does not know that he has such recourse, he probably would not want to go through an agonizing court procedure, and because the courts are usually reluctant to divide a natural family, his chances of living elsewhere are not good anyway. Juvenile court judges would often like to place the non-delinquent juvenile in insitutions other than children's prisons, but alternative arrangements simply do not exist.

This problem has been recognized for years, but because children's needs have such a low priority in our hierarchy of significant social concerns, we have not created the necessary alternatives. This is partly due to the fact that the real situation is invisible to most Americans, but it is undoubtedly also due to the deeply entrenched belief that all children should be raised with their natural parents in the nuclear family. America is almost the only society which thrusts the young couple into marriage and child rearing and expects them to do it all by themselves without family, friends, professional or domestic help, or training. Here, it has been possible only for the wealthy to extend the nuclear family by employing specially trained people to help rear their children: governesses, tutors, boarding school staff, teachers, vacation camp counselors, housekeepers, and others who lessen family responsibilities and who introduce other dimensions into a child's life through activities that his parents cannot provide. We are reluctant to provide much needed alternatives for fear that it will threaten what we feel to be an already shaky family structure, but the existence of alternatives will not necessarily lessen the viability of the nuclear family. Taking the strain off might actually help. The nuclear family should be supported. It could be a very good arrangement for many people. The problem is that it is the only domestic unit we accept.

American parents will not permit other adults, or other children for that matter, to have much contact with their children. We tend to disapprove when anyone takes any more than a distant, admiring interest in our children. We don't like to have other people care for our children, help them with their clothes, wipe their noses, let alone scold, discipline, embrace or love our children. We are so worried about perversion and pathology that we rush to our child's side if it looks as if anyone else is going to talk with him or touch him. It is a pity, because we need to find more ways to take care of each other's children if we are ever to unburden the parent from the job of constant supervision, and to provide real alternatives for the child.

If we could accept the fact that a child might experience an equally satisfactory life in an alternative home environment as he would if he spent it all with his own natural parents, then we would begin to see the possibility of many other arrangements. Unless we can accept that fact (and most people cannot) we will continue to deny the child the right to choose his own home environment.[6]

What are some viable alternatives? The first point to make of course is that there are few if any alternatives which fully honor the child's right to self-determination and none that are actually operated by children. The best known and most significant experiment in this regard is undoubtedly A. S. Neill's Summerhill, an English residential school. At Summerhill the freedom and equality of children is of paramount concern and the children's participation in the governance of the institution is fundamental to its operation. But it has proven difficult to reproduce the success of Summerhill. Both its critics and proponents agree that it is the remarkable charisma of Neill himself, his leadership in the school, and his stubborn defense of it against outside pressure that has enabled Summerhill to survive. At present, without such an indomitable figure, without such a tenacious adult buffer, it is impossible to have an alternate home environment which respects children's rights in a world which does not.

Multiple-parenting is the core concept of most alternatives now in practice. It means several adults sharing child-rearing responsibilities through community efforts, and it is comparable in its effects to natural parenting. The most famous examples are the kibbutzim in Israel. In these communes, children are raised from early infancy by women (not men) who devote their professional lives to this work. The children eat, sleep, study, and play in the "children's house," spending only a small portion of each day with their natural parents, both of whom work to maintain the kibbutz life. Parents are not expected to teach or discipline their children; their time with the children is essentially playtime, time for expressing affection, telling stories, and the like.

While there are conflicting judgments, it would appear that relationships between parents and children are exceptionally good, and the development of the children is at least comparable to the development of children raised in other more familiar ways. There is even some evidence that children of the kibbutzim perform better on tests of mental and motor development than their age-mates who have been raised elsewhere. Leslie and Karen Rabkin report this finding along with the case for child rearing in the Kibbutz:

> Kibbutz educators believe that collective education reduces parent-child conflict for several reasons: (1) the child, supported by the kibbutz, is economically independent of his parents; (2) equality of the sexes eliminates the patriarchal family system; (3) the importance of the nurse allows the child to love someone other than his parents; (4) because nurses handle the primary discipline, the daily visits of parents and children can take place under ideal conditions; (5) jealousy and anger that have to be expressed in the family can be expressed in the kibbutz because the child can find more legitimate objects of aggression among peers; and (6) the collective framework shields the child from overprotective or domineering parents who might block his efforts to become independent.[7]

A few differences between communally-raised children and those raised by a single family do appear. In the communally-raised, there seems to be a strong group ethic, a heavy dependency and loyalty to the group. The child's individual personality is sometimes submerged in group activities, and as a result, there is not the strong individualism that is found in non-communal societies. The children tend not to choose their lifetime classmates for their romantic partners as they grow older because the situation has been much more like a family and a taboo develops against sexual involvement.

Child rearing in the kibbutz requires total community commitment for which the United States has no strong ideological or nationalistic purpose. Even in Israel only 5 percent of the population have enough commitment to the experiment to actually live in kibbutzim. Erik Erikson points out that child rearing, even in families, tends to reflect national purpose, preparing children for the kind of citizenship the state seems to desire.[8]

In the search for pluralistic arrangements which permit children to live in home environments of their choice, there are additional models which should be examined. Because the kibbutzim are collective and communal and the division of labor is such as it is, the cost to the parent is not financial but rather a total dedication to the communal enterprise. On the other hand, child-care arrangements in America present a terrible financial burden, usually to the parents, sometimes to the state. The state pays for all those incarcerated in reform schools and prisons and the two hundred thousand children in foster care programs, but there should be many other realistic placement options, state supported institutions which are not just prisons. Providing such alternative residential arrangements should become the state's highest priority. For the approximately twelve thousand dollars a year it costs the state to keep one child in an institution it should be possible to provide a number of desirable alternatives. Then at least those children in most serious difficulty who cannot live at home could find someplace besides prison in which to live.

State institutions, however, cannot serve the needs of the hundreds of thousands of other families whose situations could not be considered desperate but who nevertheless do need and want alternative living arrangements. To serve these people, thoughtfully designed programs are required which (1) provide a variety of arrangements for new home environments from which to choose, (2) redistribute the costs so that neither the state nor the parents suffer the total burden, (3) make use of previously unused resources, including laymen and paraprofessionals to reduce the costs, and (4) place more choice in the hands of the child.

Social design is needed because one child or one family operating alone simply has no access to resources that give them the services they need for the price they can afford. These services and alternative environments can only be offered through the cooperative activities of large numbers of people, many of whom would like to offer services as well as obtain them. The most common example of such cooperative arrangements are informal neighborhood day care programs supervised on a rotating basis by the parents of the participating children. Because each parent, usually the mother, contributes time instead of money, the program can be maintained for little or no direct cost to the family. But there are problems with these arrangements: they usually require a highly motivated group leader to organize them, the leadership is unstable because a leader may move out of the neighborhood, there are no systematic ways of solving conflicts among the members, and the programs are usually custodial rather than recreational or educational.

To avoid the problems of informal neighborhood arrangements and to provide many new options large numbers of people could be involved in a professionally managed membership network, a kind of non-geographic community to which participants pay regular dues. Such a network would rely on the voluntary resources of its membership to solve mutual problems. With increased size come economic group benefits ranging from significantly lower fees for legal, medical, dental, psychiatric, accounting, and other professional services, to group rates on travel, insurance, consumer services and credit programs. Depending upon the interests of the members and the qualifications of the professional staff, a variety of programs could be offered based upon training and using members of the network to provide the services needed. These programs could range from counselling and child care to sex education and consciousness-raising sessions. Perhaps most importantly such a network would offer professional facilitation and management of various alternative living arrangements for its members which would be less victimizing to both parents and children. Such arrangements have of course been tried on an informal basis before, but by and large these experiments do not survive. Without a permanent membership network and a supporting professional administration even the most hopefully conceived community efforts fail.

The network concept simply holds that most people cannot now obtain the kinds of service and community support they need to improve their lives, and that these same people, given the right circumstances and appropriate professional supervision, not only can but want to offer this support and supply these services to each other. Using the network in this way provides its members with low-cost benefits that would be either unavailable or prohibitively expensive in any other setting.

Among the many possible structures which could be developed by such a network to provide alternative home environments for children are (1) multifamily communes, (2) child exchange programs, and (3) children's residences. The multifamily commune has enjoyed some recent popularity among the young, counter-culture, drop-out society, and of course has been practiced by various religious sects and other groups with strong ideological commitments for a century or more in the United States. The vast majority of such communal arrangements are temporary, seldom lasting three years. If not temporary, they tend to develop a strong autocratic leadership, a narrow ideological discipline, and often a commitment of members to each other that stems more from external attacks than to internal attractions. The reason that so many communes fail is that so many things can go wrong—from simple problems about the distribution of maintenance responsibilities to standards regarding sexual behavior to the lack of contractual arrangements for property ownership. If there were an organized network to help with these problems before the experiment begins and throughout its life, the chances for success are increased immeasurably. Children would, of course, participate fully in all aspects of the communal life. The simple fact of having more adults around than just his own mother and father expands the child's world significantly, and having the network organization acting as his advocate makes his chances for more humane treatment and greater opportunities for self-determination even better.

A second possibility of the membership network is child exchange. In such a program families would essentially swap children, children who have created a problem for the parents, or simply children who would like to have the chance to experience new situations. This alternative is much like today's foreign exchange student programs.

The problem with child exchange presently is that it is informal, and haphazard, and uncommon. One man reported in the newspapers that he was offering his child in exchange for another troublesome teenager, and within the first few days he received more than seventy responses. The interest in such arrangements is high, but professional methods to facilitate them do not now exist. Within a membership network, however, arrangements could be made so that not only would the exchanges be at the option of the children as well as at the pleasure of the parents, but counseling and contracts would also be introduced to help safeguard the system.

A third possible alternative involves residences operated by children themselves. These intentional communities, organized by the network staff and similar to those now operated by and for the elderly, would have adults in residence as consultants (or in other capacities), but would be by and large, managed by children functioning in self-determined and self-governing ways. One of the less visible problems is that the arrangement might reduce contact with older people, a condition of segregation that is already regarded by some observers as the fundamental problem for children in American society. Under present circumstances the financing for children's residences would have to come largely from the parents, and special problems such as infant care would require adult legal responsibility. But these problems are not insurmountable.

Another structure, not requiring a membership network, is the day care or day-and-night care facility. It is financed not only by parents but by the parents' employers who indirectly benefit by it. Because costs are never below seventy dollars a month and average about one hundred and fifteen dollars a month (costs for fully adequate care are usually estimated to be more than two hundred dollars a month), professional day care poses extremely difficult financial problems for most people. A single working mother earning five hundred dollars a month (taking home less) and spending another one hundred dollars for child care, simply cannot exist on her income. Unfortunately, child care is needed most by those who can afford it least.

This proposal attempts to redistribute the costs to all those who benefit from it. Because the parents benefit from child care that permits either or both of them to work, it is not unreasonable to ask them to participate in the costs. On the other hand, the parents' employer benefits too. Even the state benefits and should be partially responsible for the cost. Such multiple-source financing could bring child care into the realm of possibility for many people.

We are already beginning to see child care programs offered as fringe benefits to employees of large and small business, schools and hospitals, or as benefits of union membership. Centers are located on company property or nearby, making it possible for parents to be close to their children for frequent visits. Payment plans for such child care vary, but could be charged on an inverse scale: the low-paying jobs receiving the highest subsidy. In the future such programs could operate much as health insurance now does with the possible exception that state and federal aid might share part of the costs. Competent, inexpensive child care existing in many places and many forms cannot help but enlarge the home alternatives for children.

The main objective of all these alternatives is to make it possible for the child to exercise choice in his own living arrangements. Such choice can only come if we move toward an acceptance of the idea of pluralism in child rearing. The principle way we can provide for the right to alternative home environments is to display and make such possibilities acceptable. Until society as a whole can recognize the efficacy and value of these environments, there is litttle chance that the child will see that he does have options. And there is no chance that parents will be freed from the awesome responsibility of being a child's first, last, and only resort.

5

The Right to Responsive Design

If a visitor from another planet were to happen upon an American city that was for some reason uninhabited, he would never guess that children existed. He would think that our world was made up exclusively of people five-and-a-half to six feet tall, because the entire man-made world is designed to that scale.

Only in places that are used exclusively by children, such as classrooms, do we find facilities built to children's scale, almost nowhere else. This is further evidence that children are simply not important enough for adults to keep in mind when designing the environment.

Consider the small child's day: he begins by taking a shower under an uncontrollable waterfall pouring down from several feet overhead; he grips the edges of the toilet seat, desperately afraid that he will fall in and be washed away; he is unable to reach the cabinet or the sink and must try to see himself in a mirror placed so high that it misses him completely. No wonder he doesn't look the way we think he should. And he hasn't yet left the bathroom. Soon he must go out into the world to try to open doors that are too heavy for him, negotiate stairs that are too steep, reach items on shelves that are too high, pass through turnstiles that hit him directly in the face, find his way in confusing cafeteria lines, ride on dangerous school buses, see a film almost totally obscured by the back of the auditorium seat in front of him, get a drink out of a fountain he can't reach, make a phone call from a pay telephone placed at an adult height, sit on a swivel chair when his feet can't touch the floor, bang into sharp corners, risk his life in a revolving door. Is it any wonder that the child comes to feel that everything is made for adults; that adults are more important?

Writing in 1892, Kate Wiggins described the predicament of the small child in her book, *Children's Rights:*

> The child has a right to a place of his own, to things of his own, to surroundings which have some relation to his size, his desires, and his capabilities.
>
> How should we like to live, half the time, in a place where the piano was twelve feet tall,

> the doorknobs at an impossible height, and the mantle a shelf in the sky; where every mortal thing was out of reach except a collection of highly interesting objects on dressing tables and bureaus, guarded, however, by giants and giantesses, three times as large and powerful as ourselves, ever saying "mustn't touch"; and if we did touch we should be spanked and have no other method of revenge save to spank back symbolically on the inoffensive person of our dolls.
>
> Things in general are so disproportionate to the child's stature, so far from his organs of prehension, so much above his horizontal line of vision, so much ampler than his immediate surroundings, that there is, between him and all these things, a gap to be filled only by a microcosm of playthings which give him his first object lessons.[1]

Seeing a drinking fountain placed at a convenient height for children, however infrequently it occurs, does remind us of the presence of children. And having more such physical reminders that there are children in the world would help to make us more alert and attentive toward them, making their lives safer and more interesting. The real advance for children will come when adults recognize them as an integral part of the community, expecting them to be around, naturally looking out for them.

Forcing children to cope with an oversized world may have created hidden as well as obvious limitations for them. There is an interesting parallel in the way we treat left-handedness. Countries which provide for left-handedness tend to have much more of it than countries which do not. In the Soviet Union only 4 percent of the population is left-handed, while in the United States where we are more accepting of it, the figure is 16 percent. Compare these relatively low figures with those of Denmark where over 40 percent of the population is left-handed. In a country such as Denmark, being left-handed is not considered a negative trait, the word "sinister," meaning both evil and left, does not exist in their language, the furniture catalogues regularly list models in right- and left-handed styles, and there are as many left-handed scissors as right-handed ones. We can only assume that the responsive environment has allowed something to develop which might not otherwise have appeared. It makes one wonder what we might be missing having engineered our world to fit only adults.

The politics of childhood is clearly evident when one visits a child care center—even a newly constructed "model center" which is supposedly designed for optimal use by children. One does indeed see small tables and chairs and cabinets accessible to children, but in almost no other way is the facility designed for them. From looking at the arrangement it is apparent what the people who run the institution want the children to do—stay at their work tables and put their things away. Only the facilities necessary for these activities are designed to their scale. As in most classrooms the teacher is provided with blackboards and bulletin boards, displaying the children's work at heights reaching all the way to the ceiling but not to the floor. The areas where important decisions are made are for adults only. Children are not even admitted to, let alone accommodated in, the kitchen facilities or the administrative headquarters. The facility is designed for ease of adult supervision and control. Children are there to do the assigned curriculum and to follow the adult schedule. All decisions are made by adults, even those which affect the children directly. The politics of childhood remain the same from one institution to the next.

Facilities do exist, however, which accommodate children as well as the adults who must work with them. Such a case is the child care program at Synanon, the California based rehabilitation center for drug addicts and others desiring a new life style. In their Santa Monica facility one experiences a world designed to make life better for children. Blackboards and mirrors go all the way to the floor and the shelving is low, displaying all kinds of materials with which children can engage in fantasy play. Upon entering, an adult feels the difference immediately. Not a feeling of being a giant in a world built for much smaller people, because it is certainly not uncomfortable for an adult, but more a sense that one has never been in such a place. One realizes instantly that it is a place for children as well as adults.

The accommodation to children is particularly evident in the nursery, where children from six to eighteen months spend their time. In most facilities one would see cribs set at an adult height to make it easy to handle and control the children, and at the same time, imprisoning them and making them dependent upon the adult for freedom. Instead, at Synanon sleeping pallets on the carpeted floor make it possible for the child of any age to climb in and out of his bed and to have free access to other children and other parts of the room. The teacher is not accommodated in the traditional way but can often be found seated on the floor with the children telling stories, playing, or singing. Simple design decisions have created new freedom and mobility for the children, if not for the adults. Consistent with the rest of the design for children at Synanon, the meeting rooms where plans and decisions are made as accessible to children as adults and they participate as freely.

Unfortunately examples of bad design for children far outnumber examples of good design. The basic problem is that even the "good" examples are not always good politically because they are found only where adults think children should be. This reflects our idea that childhood should be a time of isolation from adults. Children must accommodate the adult, never vice versa. M. Paul Friedberg, the noted landscape architect who has designed some of America's most remarkable and widely acclaimed playgrounds admits that, much as he enjoys creating playgrounds, he believes that segregating children into them is not ultimately the best design solution. He holds rather that more of the world now denied to children should be made available to them. But examples of design which give children equal access to the facilities which are ordinarily thought to be only for adults are still nonexistent.

The occasional appearance of good design for children serves only to remind us how often such facilities are missing. Special zoos have been designed for children, permitting them to see clearly and to touch the animals. Doors and gates are scaled to their size, making them easy to open. This is in contrast to most zoos where the child's view is seriously impaired by fences, railings, and hedges, making it virtually impossible to see without the aid of an adult. Even in the best of children's zoos the telephones, food and drink counters, and vending machines are placed for the convenience of adults, which means that the important functions of communication and the expenditure of money are, as usual, left to adults.

One can look almost anywhere and discover that facilities for children are either absent or inadequate. Even in places where one might reasonably expect to find children, such as in stores, restaurants, and libraries, there is little responsive design. In business, industry, hospitals, theaters and other places children are totally excluded. Some restaurants do provide booster seats, high chairs, special bibs and napkins for small children, but with the exception of a few family restaurants, most cater to adults only and children are somehow out of place. Markets have shopping baskets with seats for children, but this babysitting device does more than carry the child, it prevents him from "getting into things," and keeps him a virtual prisoner.

It would be possible to redesign supermarket shelves in the form of bins mounted on a ferris wheel-like arrangement which the small child (or the handicapped person in a wheelchair) could pull down to obtain the item he desired. Instead, supermarkets now place some items such as children's cereal boxes where children can see them, and possibly knock them down, increasing the pressure on parents to buy them. Children as consumers are exploited rather than served.

The child's problem comes into focus when we examine the three-billion-dollar toy industry. For all the pleasure toys can bring, they are among the main weapons in the conspiracy against children. Toys for children did not even exist until children became segregated and adults began to develop an antipathy toward them. While there are a few examples of toys dating from ancient Egypt, it is likely that until the seventeenth century most toys were used also by adults. One of the first toys to be made exclusively for children was the hobby horse.

Both the structure and content of most toys reflect a demeaned view of children. Many toys are both dangerous and cheaply made. And because the child is denied access to the real world, toys create a miniature world in which the child can participate without threatening adults. He can play war games, or learn to cook and clean, or even engage in business—but only at the level of play. Moreover the kind of play the toys induce is limited, sexist, and unimaginative, while the advertising of the toys tends to be deceptive and exploitive.

The lack of concern for safety in toy manufacturing through the years has led manufacturers to sell ovens and irons with exposed 110-volt electrical outlets, rattles and musical toys with sharp wires, plastic airplanes with protrusions made of cheap material that splinters upon impact. There are metal casting sets that burn, chemistry sets that poison, archery sets which fire arrows capable of piercing an eyeball, unsanitary looped drinking straws that harbor bacteria, blocks covered with toxic paint, doll clothing and playthings that are highly flammable, sharp pins in dolls' hair bows, and simulated gunfire that is loud enough to produce deafness.[2]

The U.S. Public Health Service estimates that seven hundred thousand American children are hurt each year, and some killed, while using their playthings.

Many complicated and dangerous toys carry no precautionary advice, give no warnings about proper usage, and require constant adult supervision. This need for supervision keeps the child dependent and the adult burdened.

Toy manufacturers and congressional legislators

are becoming aware of the need for toy safety and many of the indictments of the toy industry have been exaggerated or are no longer true. Most of the estimated seven hundred thousand injuries, for example, probably result from the use of wheeled vehicles such as bicycles, tricycles, skate boards, wagons, and roller skates. Sleds and balls account for another significant portion of the injuries. So household toys such as dolls, ovens, and target pistols are not responsible for the majority of injuries. And under pressure from consumer advocates and congressional leaders the most dangerous of these toys have been discontinued.

The more serious problems with toys are not the safety factors but their social and psychological impact, and these problems tend to be less visible.[3]

So-called serial toys, Barbie dolls, for example, require major expenditures for elaborate sets of clothes, "friends," and equipment, all of which have a highly specialized purpose and limit the use of imagination and fantasy. They tend to reflect sexist ideas of what little girls should be. The emphasis is on attracting a male and developing a beauty-queen concept of what a woman should be. Boys are given the same treatment with GI Joe dolls, which come with all kinds of weapons and accessories for battle, or other forms of masculine activity.

Too often toys are used as babysitters. Giving a child a toy is like telling him to watch television. Toys can also convey a materialistic view of life, selling the child on the American ideal that accumulating things is the path to happiness. And the toy store's arsenal of weaponry and its glamourization of war, its training for violence, and its development of a cops-and-robber mentality in children is all too well known.

Although there are some new legal restraints on the manufacture and advertising of toys, it cannot be said that any major improvements are likely to come in the way of toys made or sold. But making the world safe and accessible to children is a challenge worthy of the talents of toy manufacturers. If they put themselves on the side of children politically, the books, films, and television programs they control could help raise the consciousness and the power of children. Now their efforts are almost entirely in the opposite direction.

Millions of dollars are now spent on television advertising for children, all too often making toys seem something other than what they are. The child's disappointment when the toy does not live up to expectations is such an old story with parents that some even argue this may be the best education of all: to learn not to trust what people tell you on television.

The nation's leading group working to improve television for children is ACT, Action for Children's Television. They have fought to reduce the number of commercials presented during children's programs, to upgrade the quality of programming, to reduce the amount of violence shown, and to force advertisers to be more truthful. In addition, they are trying to prevent the hosts of children's shows from personally delivering commercial messages. Remarkable progress has been made, despite the many obstacles.[4]

ACT, however, is more committed to the protection of children than to the protection of their rights. The strategy for the liberation of children is undermined by such paternalistic protection of children. If, for example, adults are going to receive commercial advertisements, then so should children. It would be against the political interests of the child to remove all commercials from children's programming without doing the same for adults. Eliminating commercials for children would not only reinforce the ability of children's programming to create a children's television ghetto and further reinforce the low opinion of children held by programmers, but it would also systematically deny them the consumer information they may need to function as fully participating members of society.

Another project supported by ACT is to encourage parents to turn off television on Saturdays (TOTS). The idea of a parent forbidding a child to watch a favorite program should be as outrageous to us as a child doing that to his parent. The parental decision to prevent a child from watching what he desires to watch introduces a double standard and deprives the child of his rights.

Children's programming is whatever children want to see. They do not now have the need, the interest or the opportunity to watch much of what adults enjoy watching. With the advent of children's liberation that might change. Children are now dulled by watching hour after hour of cheaply made animated cartoons—full of violence—whose only value is their ability to keep the glazed eyes of the child riveted on the set, ready only for the next commercial message. One might speculate that often the reason children choose the animated program is not only that it is more attention-getting and violent, but because they have been conditioned to believe that animated programs "belong" to them, while live-action programs "belong" to adults. Hopefully some day all of television will belong to children as much as it does to adults. We may then see the design of programming more genuinely responsive to children.

One proposal worth studying is not to decommercialize children's programming but to decommercialize television. If television were noncommercial, it would not have to be so blatantly attention-getting. The ability to keep people watching has little to do with the quality of the programming. It is quite possible, even likely, that the quality of television could be improved and yet become at the same time less demanding and magnetic. Then both adults and children could be more discriminating in its use, perhaps setting aside some of the twenty-seven hours a week that the child spends in front of the TV set as time for adults and children to be together.

Toys and television and the lack of facilities in children's scale offer only the most obvious examples, from very different media, of both failures and possibilities in what we generally regard as the field of design. But there is also the broader issue of our responsiveness to the needs of children in the area of social design, most notably in dealing with children's right to adequate health care and to physical mobility.

Considering the fact that we are supposed to be a child-oriented nation, our children are given very poor health care. There are thirteen nations ranking ahead of us in their ability to prevent infant mortality. Between six hundred thousand and a million babies are born each year to mothers who receive no medical care—prenatal, delivery, or postnatal. Probably one-half of all women in low income brackets receive little or no prenatal care. Most poor children never see a dentist throughout their childhood. There are twelve million children with eye problems, two million with orthopedic problems, and three million with speech impediments. Five and one-half million are handicapped and only a third of them receive any educational assistance. There are eight hundred thousand emotionally-disturbed children, only thirteen percent of whom receive special education. One million four hundred thousand children under eighteen needed psychological care in 1966 but only one-third received it.[5] Only about half of the children in the

United States are properly immunized again disease.

The problem is not restricted to the poverty stricken, but it is certainly most severe there. The extent of nutritional deficiencies in American children is largely unknown, but the average child on public assistance is allotted only forty dollars a month, and it is clearly difficult to feed him adequately, let alone to provide first-rate health care for him on that amount. Health care has become a monstrous problem not just for children but for everyone. We must find ways of breaking through the professional barriers to a solution that works for all members of our society.

With respect to children's rights, perhaps the most important change in health care should be the child's right to obtain medical treatment on his own, without parental consent. This right should not be construed to mean that the physician is empowered to dictate the kind of treatment a child receives without having to explain it to the parent, but rather that the child is empowered to deal directly with the physician and to have some freedom and responsibility in the actions taken with respect to his own health. In cases where the child is unable to seek medical attention on his own he should of course be represented by a parent or advocate. The child should be given complete information on his condition and on the procedures that are suggested for his treatment. Beyond this, children need information on a variety of health problems, notably those of birth control and venereal disease. Adopted children must also have the right to obtain their natural family's medical history.

A major problem in the design of health delivery systems has been to make them responsive to the needs of children. It should no longer be possible to design a system which disregards the right of the child to have some measure of control over decisions made regarding his health. He should not only be provided for, but ought to be a part of the planning that ultimately determines the type of health care necessary. Most systems are designed for adults; health care is no exception. The child has little freedom or autonomy, and is excluded from the decision-making process.

Another example of a system that not only excludes children but is positively designed against them is transportation, the whole problem of a child's mobility. Children cannot move about in safety. They must always be under the watchful eyes of their parents or of some other responsible adult, because to leave them on their own is to invite injury or death. The child cannot easily make forays into the community and his parent lives in continual anxiety about the child's well-being.

The villain, of course, is the automobile and the many accommodations we have made to it. The automobile is the number one enemy of children. It has transformed our villages into sprawling, polluted cities and made pedestrian travel useless, difficult, and dangerous. Each year it kills fifty-seven thousand people in the United States and injures over a million others. More than any other single factor, the automobile has changed the way we live and the way we relate to each other.

The automobile first made possible, and now makes necessary, the separation of work centers from commercial, residential, and recreational centers, requiring a mobility which the child and, unfortunately, many others in our society simply do not have.[6]

Because automobiles can only be legally operated by an adult, the child is made more dependent. They are so lethal that only children over seven or eight are permitted to go anywhere on foot or bicycle; even then there is still much for the parents to worry about. While automobiles increase the mobility of adults, they reduce the mobility of children. Automobiles actually prevent children from exploring their world and from safely joining in the activities of the community.

To provide for the child's mobility we must build cities with children in mind and devise transportation systems that work for them. This is no easy task. Mass transit systems are difficult to design and difficult to sell because of our commitment to high-speed automobile travel. This design problem demands the most wrenching and large-scale changes. It means reducing our use of and reliance on the automobile. It means reorienting our work, play, family life, and commercial activities so that they are all close to each other. Reducing our need for automobiles or at least for second cars in this way, would have the additional benefit of developing stronger communities, more interpersonal activities, greater involvement, and improved safety on the streets.

In addition to urban sprawl and polluted air, the automobile has created an American life style which now demands that one commute, meaning more time away from family. It has forced Americans to carry expenses which often exceed their rent or house payments. Sometimes several hundred dollars each month must be set aside for automobile costs. It has compelled Americans to be dependent on the automotive industry which penetrates approximately 25 percent of all areas of our economy.

Our devotion to the automobile, in addition to our dependency on it, has placed it in a position of priority over children. More time and money is spent on automobiles than on children. More space is given to them. Recent laws in Sweden manage to give the same rights to children as to cars, to utilize the space near apartment complexes equally. America does not even have these minimal priorities.

Most of the proposed solutions to the problem of safety for children are respectful of the automobile: such things as overpasses and underpasses, crosswalk guards, marked crossings, traffic signals, cul-de-sacs, pedestrian walkways which connect the child's home with school and stores. Some of these solutions are helpful but carry with them their own limitations. Overpasses and underpasses are expensive and cause the additional worry of crime. Crossing guards are helpful, but it is a hazardous duty. Until Americans are using bicycles in great numbers, there will not be adequate provisons to make bicycle travel safe. In new housing developments the pedestrian walkways that permit children to walk to schools and parks without crossing streets seem to be a good solution but in practice bring a number of problems. Because Americans are so committed to building fences and walls to separate themselves from their neighbors, to guarantee privacy and the boundaries of their own property, we have transformed what could be beautiful pathways into walled alleys where children are bullied or robbed by other children. Too often, adults have had to be posted in these corridors to supervise so that fights and thefts would not occur. The necessity of this kind of surveillance defeats one of the main purposes of the walkway.

Pedestrian travel has become useless and dangerous. Rational efforts to reduce the danger have led to marked crosswalks, traffic signals and signs, but reliance on rational methods is unwise. One look at the statistics would help us realize why these techniques will not work: 39 percent of all pedestrian deaths involve people known to have been drinking; 43 percent are children under the age of four; and 36 percent of the deaths are people over the age of sixty-five. Based on this information, it is clear that almost all pedestrian deaths involve people for whom rational methods, signals and signs, would not be appropriate; they are for one reason or another unable to respond to them. This means that for safe pedestrian travel it will be necessary to "people proof" the system, making it impossible for people to walk in front of automobiles. The implications are that we will have to put automobiles where there are no people or put people where there are no automobiles. Most important, however, is the need to change our attitudes so that automobiles are secondary to pedestrians.

Our world has not been made to fit children; adult facilities do not work for them. The argument that children will some day be adults and will then have full use of these facilities only underscores our attitude that childhood is not important in itself but only as a developmental period for adults-in-training. A person's childhood, however, lasts for many years, almost an entire generation. A long time to ask him to wait. Even more significant, there *always* will be millions of children, a third of our population, incapacitated in a world not built to fit them.

6

The Right to Information

A child's ignorance is a strong political ally of adult society, and adults have learned to rely heavily on it. Even the institutions that are designed to educate and inform children serve double duty by also keeping them ignorant and dependent. Denying children information "to protect them from the harsh realities of life" has been common practice for so long that now adults simply cannot recognize a child's right to the truth. Adults are so accustomed to giving mythical or simplistic answers to children's questions—to censoring what they see, hear, and read, to distorting the facts to suit adult purposes—that one wonders that children ever gain information.

The most serious denials of information to children come from our perceptions about the nature of childhood. For the most part, we don't think much about children's need for information and don't believe that we should have to make special provisions for them to enter our world. As a result children are denied information by being denied access to adult life, and in turn are denied access to adult life by being denied information.

They are excluded from almost every institution in our society and have no way of finding out what it is they might need to know in order to gain potency. They are separated from the adult world, barred from important conversations, prevented from being where decisions are made, and excluded from social gatherings, dinner parties, and business meetings. Women have now come to recognize how being excluded from businessmen's luncheon clubs where the power elite of the business world plan and decide, has systematically denied them access to the kinds of information they need to gain leadership positions. The same kind of exclusion takes place with children, only more so.

Paradoxically, in the very institutions which are designed to provide information to children we find the most serious prohibitions against them. Libraries are a prime example. Although most librarians are deeply concerned about a child's right to read, libraries are still a political instrument of the society and therefore extremely vulnerable to pressure to limit the kinds of books that are placed on the library shelves. This public pressure forces libraries to stock only safe, non-controversial and often mediocre materials. Censorship is inevitable in libraries where there is fear that certain documents will produce public outrage. This form of censorship has produced the most incredible incidents.

The children's book *Lassie Come Home* was removed from the shelf of one library because it referred to a female dog as a "bitch." Practically every major literary figure has been censored: Shakespeare, Hemingway, Twain—the list reads like a Who's Who of classic and contemporary literature. Very often pressure from a single group or even a single individual is enough to remove a book from the shelf. Most libraries have a special room where they can put such books. These books are usually taken out of the card catalog, as well as off the shelf, so that no one knows that the library actually has a copy. This kind of censorship observes no double standard, denying adults as well as children, but its rationale is the protection of children's innocence.

The most common prohibitive technique is of course self-censorship. This means that libraries simply don't order controversial materials in the first place. Most libraries, for example, do not subscribe to *Playboy,* even though it is one of America's leading magazines.

Libraries differ in the techniques they use in dealing with children. Sometimes special library cards are issued which are good only in the children's section of the library. The periodical rooms, which house the magazines and newspapers and other materials of current interest, are ordinarily off limits to children. In the Los Angeles Public Library some books are marked with red tape, a signal to the librarian that the child is not to have the book without written permission from his parents. Other systems require librarians to interrogate the child who asks for a book as to his interest in it. Even if a child can find out about a book and ask for it by name, there is a good chance he won't be able to obtain it because the librarian may decide that a child should not be interested in that subject.

In the 1950's the pressure for censorship came mainly from the political right, in attempts to ban books that were thought to be sexually obscene or unpatriotic. Now the pressure is from the left to remove materials held to be racist or sexist, discriminating against the oppressed peoples in our society. If one expects to find erotic books in the libraries' censored material, he will be disappointed. The books censored for sexual content are books like Maurice Sendak's *In the Night Kitchen,* which shows frontal nudity of a small boy, or a Time-Life book, *How Babies Are Made,* which shows animals copulating. And he is even more likely to find the original versions of *Little Black Sambo* and *Epaminondas* censored because of their demeaning portrayals of blacks.

Much as we deplore the oppression of minority groups we cannot use censorship of children's reading material to end discrimination against them.

If we do, it will eventually backfire. For example, the focus of current pressure for censorship is turning from racist literature to sexist literature. Moreover, we are coming to see that there are many other oppressed groups in our society. In one sense everyone belongs to an oppressed group. If we were to respond to all of the pressures from such groups, we would have to take every book off the shelf, for every one contains references to groups who are now, or who soon will be, demanding an end to their oppression. If one were trying to eliminate all of the demeaning references to children in literature it becomes immediately clear just how impossible the task of book burning would become.

We cannot protect civil rights by ending them. The alternative to taking every book off the shelves is to put the books on the shelves, books that make the invisible oppression more visible. The rule should be better books, not fewer books—information, not censorship.[1]

One of the major concerns of librarians is the mediocrity of children's literature.[2] Because people think that children are not discriminating, most children's books are written for extraliterary purposes, for the "children's market." The writing always seems condescending and superficially optimistic.[3] Children do not warrant such protection, first because they are not innocent, and second, because it inevitably leads to innocuous, noncontroversial and unstimulating literature. Unfortunately, children will accept almost any book, perhaps for the reason suggested by one of the characters in Decker's *An Empty Spoon,* "I like books because they are the only things that don't tell you you are stupid."[4] It is a pity to note that his statement is only relatively true. Children's books do tell you you are stupid, but they do it so much less than other forces in the lives of children.

As middle-of-the-road and noncontroversial as libraries may be, they present an extremely broad range of information compared to the limited information that comes to the child through the compulsory education system. The child spends his entire day in school looking at state-controlled material that, because it must be acceptable to everyone, is hopelessly bland. Although in the average school the teacher talks 80 percent of the time, what he or she is able to say is so narrowly prescribed by the government that there is almost no opportunity for the exploration of subjects which are most interesting to children—sex and death, for example.[5]

The most lamentable denial of information in the school system occurs not because of the limited curriculum but because of the limited intellectual interests of the faculty. Curiously, teaching does not usually attract the intellectually disposed. Nothing in teacher training creates in teachers an excitement about learning. Nothing in the professional development of teachers is likely to make them better at informing students than they were before they began their college education. What is worse, societal pressures to conform have so restricted them that they can't even use what they know very effectively. As a result of being with many of these people our children emerge from school not only poorly informed but uninterested in learning.

Student's school records provide examples of two different problems relating to children's right to information. First, they represent a source of information to which the child does not have access. And second, they illustrate the way in which information about a child over which he has no control can be used without his knowledge and thereby invade his privacy.

A study by the Russell Sage Foundation on information collected in schools presents a serious indictment of the procedures used.[6] Information about the students may be gathered for one purpose but used for quite another. It is almost always compiled without the consent of either the child or the parent and neither has any information about what is in the file and what use is to be made of it. Information including IQ scores, teacher's or counselor's reports, personality data, and health records are systematically withheld from both parent and child. The secrecy of this system prohibits the careful evaluation of the accuracy of such information and in any case neither parent nor child is permitted to challenge any of it. Worst of all, these records are cumulative and permanent and there is no practice of their systematic destruction. Unauthorized personnel, from a teacher who might not have any legitimate interest to a policeman who may be able to use the material against a child, have access to the file even if they cannot demonstrate a need for the information. The information is not protected from subpoena and is usually available for any research purpose. All this represents a tremendous threat to individual privacy and to the liberation of the child. It is time to completely rethink what kinds of records should be kept, the purposes to which they should be put, and, most particularly, the ownership and management of these records.

An argument can be made for maintaining certain kinds of identifying records—for instance, a child's home telephone number for use in case of an emergency—but when the benefits are weighed against the evils, it is not at all clear that *any* other information is desirable to keep on file. Not even the phone number should be there unless the child gives such consent. The disadvantages of the system of record keeping are much greater than the advantages. As a consequence of this system, students are labelled and categorized, secretly placed on tracks toward college or vocational training, and damaged by derogatory material which appears on their permanent files as the result of temporary anger or prejudiced teachers. The serious flaws of all diagnostic measures recorded in these files, the invalidity of psychological tests used, the fact that having certain knowledge and therefore certain expectations of children tends to be self-confirming, the way in which test scores prejudice teachers and administrators all combine to make the keeping of records a highly questionable procedure.

This infringement on the rights of children is not an insignificant problem, and even though the elimination of educational records would cause great difficulty, we simply must make major changes and sacrifices in their behalf. In so doing we may not be able to accommodate existing educational practices and philosophies. Record keeping is related to the educational philosophy of diagnosing a child, programming him toward goals that are established by others, making sure that he learns the material required by the state. If on the other hand self-directed learning is the major goal, the possession of records by school authoritites becomes less important, if not totally inappropriate.

No records should be kept other than those the child himself wishes to keep. He should own and manage his own file. Access to the file should be obtained with his permission only and nothing should be added to it without his consent. Because he owns it he would never have to resort to challenging the information. If this plan proves too radical, we could at least make *some* changes in the present system that would empower children. Certainly children should have access to their files, be able to challenge the information that is in them, and control the access of outside people to them.

Information about people that is designed to go into computerized data banks should simply not be collected on individuals per se. It will, of course, be necessary for certain kinds of information to be gathered just to enable educators and administrators to engage in realistic planning, but it is *not* absolutely necessary that the material be gathered in a way that identifies individuals. Planning on both a large and small scale can be done anonymously with random sampling techniques.

Most record keeping is aimed at clustering children who have similar test scores. Clustering is a questionable educational practice in itself, and if the inability to place children in homogeneous clusters is part of the price we pay to enable children to be liberated from the evils of cumulative records, it will be well worth it.

It is important to place oneself in the position of the child in whose cumulative file exist such scribbled comments by former teachers as "lazy," "has filthy health habits," "seems effeminate, possible homosexual tendencies," and so forth. A child should be able to erase such information. And perhaps teachers should not be allowed to write it.

Children are also prevented from seeing certain films, plays, and television programs which presumably carry information that society does not want children to have. Excessive violence does not seem to be one of the concerns, for the average child sees literally thousands of filmed and televised murders. We do, however, seem to want to keep sexual matters out of the child's thoughts, and so there are movies that are unavailable because the theater manager prevents him from attending, and movies that are unavailable because his parents prevent him from attending. To say nothing of the price of admission that prevents him from attending some movies. The lack of financial resources cannot be discounted as a major obstacle to gaining information.

Television works its own kind of censorship by scheduling most of the adult programming so that it is presented after children have gone to bed. Because television generally offers only what is fit for children to see, it presents a good example of the way in which adults suffer from censorship that is actually directed at children.

The right to information can protect a child's right to privacy as we have seen with respect to school record keeping. It does not mean on the other hand that a child has the license to intrude on the privacy of others to obtain information. Because a child wants information about sex does not mean he should be able to invade his parents' bedroom. Certainly no one need answer a question that seems like a violation of one's private thoughts just because a child has asked it. Adults and children alike should have control over their private lives. If any privacy needs protection, however, it is the child's. Adults think nothing of entering a child's private space—if indeed he has a private space—of opening his mail, going through his drawers, interrogating him about his associates or his activities.

As a result, most children have no private lives.

A parent's interest in the life and thoughts of his child is of course desirable, and he certainly should feel that he could ask about them. But children, like adults, should have the right not to answer.

Parents have always felt that it is best to keep certain kinds of information secret from children, and surely there are privacies in any relationship that should be privileged. Many times, however, the information is withheld because the parents don't want to worry the child or burden him with knowledge which he might not protect with the same secrecy that they would. Very often this secrecy involves information about how the family is operating, possible job changes, economic conditions, moving arrangements, making major financial outlays, marital difficulties, plans for the children, and so on. This information cannot be denied children if they are to participate fully and helpfully in family matters. This is particularly true with respect to the possibility of imminent divorce. The decision to dissolve a family has always been an adult decision and most of the information relevant to that decision is withheld from the children. When the effects of family break up are as great on the children as on the parents, and generally they are, then children should not only know about what is happening, but should be in on the decision, and their desires and needs with respect to custody should be honored as a matter of children's rights.

Subjecting children to the prohibitions and deceptions which keep them uninformed and dependent ultimately threatens our democratic process, which requires above all else an informed citizenry. The most potent weapon against tyranny is knowledge that is accessible to all members of society. Whenever one group decides what is and what is not desirable for another to know, whenever a "we-they" condition exists, society becomes vulnerable to totalitarianism. For this reason, among many others, laws, policies, or regulations should not prevent children from acquiring information of all kinds, especially the kind that makes adults most uncomfortable. One of the reasons this information causes adults distresss is because it empowers children, making it less easy to control and dominate them.

As always it is our attitude toward children which determines what kind of information they get. Our predisposition to ignore their concerns, deal expeditiously with their questions, and deny them entry into the world of adults keeps them ignorant, dependent, and impotent.

7

The Right to Educate Oneself

The only people in our society who are incarcerated against their will are criminals, the mentally ill, and children in school. Of those, school children are by far the largest group, sixty-three million. They are incarcerated for a longer time than criminals or the mentally ill in institutions which are, in Charles Silberman's words, "joyless, repressive and mindless."[1]

The child has no choice. In every state except Mississippi compulsory attendance at school is the law. Children and their parents can be arrested for noncompliance. The alternative to school is jail. But even with such an unpleasant alternative, children have been known to choose jail over attending school.

Schools are made compulsory not only by our

laws but by other mechanisms as well. If they do not complete their schooling, students are threatened with unemployment, poverty, and exclusion from society.

A hope began with our founding fathers that with free, tax-supported public education available to everyone, a literate and informed populace would develop, a people capable of self-government. While that hope still burns brightly, it has been translated into a system of compulsory attendance at school which is having a very different effect. The enforced, threatening quality of education in America has taught people to hate school, to hate the subject matter, and tragically, to hate themselves.

The manner in which subjects are taught derives its power not from its intrinsic appeal to children but more from the fact that they are compelled to sit through it. As James Hearndon has illustrated, children, given the choice, would rather be someplace other than the classroom and the "success" of some teaching efforts is actually based upon the fact that they do not have that choice. The success is only relative to the dismal experiences children have in other classrooms.[2]

We like to think that people do learn something in school, but the results are disappointing to say the least. We believe that children in school learn to read when in fact they learn *not* to read. The average child is so averse to reading by the time he has finished his compulsory education that he seldom picks up a book after graduation. Fifty-seven percent of all high school graduates surveyed in a Gallup poll had not read a book within the previous year.[3]

Not only have students failed to learn the subject matter pertinent to self-government, but in the authoritarian and arbitrary system of American education they have not experienced it either. Compulsory education and the autocracy fostered by it has robbed children of any sense of what independence of action and freedom of choice might be.[4] School has made the concept of participation in the decisions that affect them so remote to students that the real lesson in compulsory education is that one cannot be trusted to govern oneself.

The movement to abolish compulsory education is gaining momentum and is being vigorously debated by growing numbers of people in our nation. Many leading educators, particularly those no longer teaching, have come out strongly against it. Some see the evils of compulsory education to be so great that they advocate de-schooling society altogether, starting over from scratch. But what will children do if they are not compelled to go to school? Immediately one imagines scenes of chaos, children in revolutionary bands wandering aimlessly, playing endlessly, not accomplishing or achieving, not contributing. The images that come to our mind say more about our own beliefs about the basic nature of man than about the probable consequences of de-schooling.

Without doubt, ending compulsory education will change a great many institutions other than education itself. It raises the prospect of children working, entering the labor force at an early age. It changes our idea of home and family, of child care and parental responsibility. Again, it is impossible to change one element of the system without experiencing widespread systemic change.

Because most educators, and educational reformers for that matter, take compulsory education for granted, one can assume that whatever changes are made will be made within that framework. Not enough thought has yet been given to what might be done if attendance at school were not required, nevertheless some interesting alternatives have been suggested.

In a category which might be called mild reform are those proposals suggested by John Holt, who advocates abolishing compulsory education but tries pragmatically to offer a number of steps that might be taken short of that goal.[5] He suggests that we might reduce the number of days of required attendance. Or if one hundred and eighty days were required, a child might simply have his school attendance ticket validated that many times during the year. Another possibility for the student would be to complete the entire one hundred and eighty days in ninety days by attending double sessions. Evening schools might be created to give opportunity and credit for apprenticeship training and other work activities. One might attend more than one school during any one given period of time.

Christopher Jencks proposes the use of educational entitlements, expenditures made by the students in the public or private schools of their choice. Similarly Paul Goodman, Milton Friedman and others have proposed voucher systems that would permit the child, with parental guidance to spend his money in the institution he thought would best educate him. Such systems, in addition to giving the child and parent greater discretion in planning educational experiences, would also reduce the disadvantages of the poor and other groups now denied quality education because of the requirements of attending school within their own segregated neighborhoods.

More controversial suggestions come from men like Ivan Illich who advocates the use of an "edu-credit card." Issued at birth, this card would permit entrance into many different learning resources, not all of which would be schools.[6] A variety of institutions in the community could qualify for edu-credit reimbursement. Programs suitable for different kinds of educational activities could be developed in museums, libraries, hospitals, factories, banks, construction firms, theater companies, photography studios, stock brokerages, office buildings, lumber yards, insurance companies, labor unions, professional groups, sports stadiums, or newspaper plants.[7] Almost all community resources, stores, and businesses, from the telephone company to a bakery could offer important learning experiences, not only in the specific details and larger problems of that particular organization, but in reading dials, telling time, keeping records, measuring, alphabetizing, counting, and so on through most of what we think of as basic skills. In addition, special schools could be developed around a particular theme such as bilingual training, science, art, and physical education which might attract certain students. Schools and other institutions which qualify for reimbursement would essentially compete for students. The more attractive alternatives would no doubt receive the larger number of applications. Attractiveness is, of course, no guarantee of quality, but unattractiveness is usually indicative of something wrong.

Holt and others suggest giving cash directly to the student or family for expenditure in whatever way they consider helpful to the learning experience of the child. Whatever failings it might have, this system is one way of giving cash directly to the poor. The number one problem of most poverty programs is that the money somehow never gets to the poor people, having been siphoned off by bureaucrats, researchers, and social workers. This plan also avoids the insult implied by voucher systems, which, like food stamps, assume that the person receiving the money might not spend it in the way that it is intended for him to spend it.

Even more radical suggestions circumvent professional educators altogether by proposing networks of laymen, children and adults forming what Illich calls learning webs, connections between people which enable them to learn from each other whatever it may be that one cares to learn and another is capable of teaching. These learning webs could be formal, institutionalized and relatively permanent arrangements or they could be informal, spontaneous and temporary. The point is that there are many untapped educational resources in any community which if linked with people interested in learning would provide alternatives to the present educational system.

No educational reformer who has been around for any length of time expects education to change much—certainly not rapidly. They all know better. Trying to change education is like kicking a big mountain of mashed potatoes. It seems easy enough to make a dent, but somehow the mountain just stays there.

Time and again educational consultants have been seduced by their success in producing small and temporary changes. This has led a number of them to believe that education could indeed be altered, perhaps even changed fundamentally with new ideas and experimental demonstration programs in classrooms and individual schools. Surely, they thought, good ideas supported by research data and demonstration programs would become contagious, spreading throughout the educational establishment.

Needless to say, that never happened. Usually the new program would begin with a great deal of enthusiasm in a single classroom or an individual school, and then after a period of time, would just fade away. That has happened with the best of ideas. The most innovative, thoughtful, well-staffed programs ultimately fail.

Realizing that the problem was not a lack of good ideas, the consultants decided that he problem was implementation. Perhaps if teachers had opened up to the possibilities of change, if their attitudes had been altered, their resistance overcome, then the good ideas could have been implemented. Acting on this hypothesis, the problem was approached through massive applications of sensitivity training, group encounters, gaming and role playing, simulations, and other in-service education for teachers. The teachers, for the most part, were willing and cooperative, but all this training simply made their efforts in applying their new insights more frustrating when they encountered opposition from the people who ran their respective systems.

It was then generally conceded that the problem was one of organizational development. Perhaps the rigid administrative hierarchies, the dead weight of bureaucracy, the fears of upper level bureaucrats, the interdepartmental conflicts, and the lack of communication, were the main problems. Consultants began working on intergroup relations, conflict management, organizational goal setting—again without success. Attempts to bring about fundamental change escalated further to intensive consultation with top leadership in each of the school systems in the hope that using the power of their high office, administrators could facilitate the new designs for education that were otherwise blocked. Still no real change.

Consultants were able to maintain their high motivation through all this because the immediate results of the consulting experiences were so often encouraging. The training seemed to be exciting to the teachers—they seemed willing to be innovative—and the programs that were started were well received by the students, but the educational enterprise seemed to remain intact through it all, essentially the same in every way. The history of the war between the educational reformers and the educational establishment is something like the history of smaller nations fighting wars with China. Each small nation would "win," believing itself the victor, but the immensity of China would prevail: the new victor would be enveloped while China remained.

As many of the battle-worn reformers have discovered, the main reason that educational reform has been a reform in consciousness only and not in practice is that it has been based on the faulty assumption that the educational system of today doesn't work. It was assumed that because students learn so little, because they were so dominated and shamed, because schools were so inhumane, such terrible places to grow people that the system wasn't working. The reformers thought it should matter to all of us that the many years of effort put in by the students were for the most part wasted because by the time they graduated they had lost almost all the information that they were supposed to have learned. They thought that because almost no one could solve a simple algebraic problem or pass a seventh grade history exam or even care about intellectual concerns, that the learning process was somehow failing. That was their big mistake. They didn't realize that at a more fundamental level, the educational process was working. They thought that it was dysfunctional, when actually it was highly functional. That is why it has been and will be so difficult to change.

The educational system functions not to educate children, but to maintain the system. It has not been concerned with humane learning and growth, but with keeping our way of life intact: keeping the child in his place, socially, politically, and economically. It has indoctrinated him with the values, if not the information, Americans are expected to learn.

First of all, school has been a babysitter. School is the place where we want children to be; we don't want them anywhere else. School serves that custodial function extremely well by incarcerating children almost all day, every day.

Children are programmed, channeled, tracked, credentialized, and certified in the process of stamping out standardized educational products which will be acceptable to the world into which they graduate—that of the university, the military, the worlds of business and industry, and community. Whatever the child may or may not have learned in the process is secondary to his having gained a diploma and the attitude that school is important and that those who have been schooled are superior.

In the least visible and perhaps the most profound of its functions American education marks the child indelibly with the values important to the American public. However poorly the child may learn the basic subjects taught in the regular curriculum, he will certainly learn the lessons within the hidden curriculum. This is because the hidden curriculum is not taught by the pedagogy, but by the ritual of education. The process itself teaches certain fundamental values. Among these are the importance of competition and the corollary idea that the world is comprised of winners and losers, of which, naturally, there must be a great many more of the latter. Other implied values are the idea of mindless patriotism which permits no examination, or question, or criticism of the policies of our government; concepts of sex; what boys should be and what girls should be, what they should and should not do together, what life goals are appropriate for boys or for girls; the importance of the profit system, free enterprise and the corporation in America; the idea that some work is worth money and other work, such as homemaking, is not worth money; the concept of beauty exemplified by homecoming queens and kings; the idea that progress and growth are synonymous; the underscoring of the citizen as consumer; the notion that almost anything can and should be measured; the expectations of "the good life," which differ little from the most crass, materialistic displays on television. This is what children learn in school, and unlike their course in albegra, they don't forget it.

At a time when we need acceptance of diversity, we teach uniformity.[8] In the guise of "individualized" instruction, each individual student is programmed toward a common goal. Individualized instruction has come to mean an individual approach to standardization, so that although one child may need to learn tactilely, another visually, they both eventually learn the same thing. If we could recast our thinking about individualized instruction, we could actually have individualized approaches to individualized goals.

As with just about everything else this entire system is most severely damaging to the poor. Educational failures are most evident in our treatment of minority groups and the poverty population. George Dennison, Nat Hentoff, John Holt, Ivan Illich, James Hearndon, Jonathan Kozol, Paolo Friere,[9] among others, have documented the way in which our educational system holds out a promise to the poor, but by its very nature, militates against them.

By leading a poor person to believe that he can pull himself out of poverty by getting a good education, a diploma, or a certificate, we make the possession of a diploma increasingly important. Raising standards and adding further graduate programs in an endless chain of what has been called diplomatism inevitably favors the white upper classes whose access to graduate schools and to advanced degrees is far easier. The real effect on the poor has been to put the needed diploma further out of reach and to make the lower order certificates less helpful in obtaining employment and anything else our society has to offer. So instead of working *for* the poor, education has actually worked *against* them by making the gap between the rich and the poor even wider.

Poor children attend school hoping to improve their lives and instead find the situation to be threatening, embarrassing, and insulting. They come away feeling ignorant and worthless. George Dennison makes the point that poor children in such circumstances often leave school not knowing some of the things they knew when they entered.

The right to educate oneself also has to mean freedom from indoctrination. It is necessary to distinguish between indoctrination on the one hand and the inevitable transfer of values from adult to child on the other. There is no way to avoid, nor is it desirable to avoid, the child's learning about the values of his parents and teachers. People can't help but influence others even if they try not to. Indoctrination, on the other hand, has less to do with the content of what is being taught than with method. If punishment, fear, or shame are used as sanctions, we are guilty of exploiting the weakness of children in order to impose our values on them.

Children are seen as fair game for the imposition of almost any value system held by an adult who works or lives with them. As Bertrand Russell says, "One of the few rights remaining to parents in the wage earning class is that of having their children taught any brand of superstition that may be shared by a large number of parents in the same neighborhood." [10] This is seen as an inviolate parental right. As a result, countless children experience a rape of the mind. They are compelled to learn the most outrageous, mythical and superstitious doctrines, and dogma that will incapacitate, threaten, and fill them with guilt for the rest of their lives.

The worst situations center around the teaching of religion. Fanatical parents have been known to thrust their children's hands into open fires to let them experience the pain of hellfire. Children are whipped when they don't pray in a way that will suit their parents. But most children are not physically tortured as a way of guaranteeing that they perpetuate certain adult-imposed values and beliefs. Other forms of indoctrination are more subtle, with psychological sanctions applied to make children feel stupid or guilty or fearful unless they believe and act in the ways that conform to parental values.

Invisible doctrines or value systems are always present and whatever fundamental image or view of man we hold comes through in our behavior and is indeed taught to others. For this reason it is impossible and for other reasons it is undesirable to prevent indoctrination by attempting to limit the content of adult-child conversations. The limitation can however, be placed on the methods employed. If coercion is ruled out, indoctrination in the narrow sense cannot take place. In most school, church, and family situations the child has no choice but to be there—he is not a volunteer but a captive. Until we can guarantee the child's fundamental right to opt out of these situations, precautions must be taken to make sure that the child at least experiences alternatives to the values being taught.

Freedom from indoctrination means that children choose whatever belief system comforts and inspires them, not necessarily the systems that adults would have them choose. Eli Chesen, in his book *Religion May Be Hazardous to Your Health* describes how the indoctrination of pre-school age children with abstract religious concepts and images inhibits them from relating satisfactorily to their own experiential world. This, Chesen believes, often results in serious psychological confusion for the child and prepares the ground for later mistrust of parents and other adults.

Adults' abilities to indoctrinate children are being reduced by unprecedented events taking place in our society, most notably what might be called the reverse transmission of culture, what Margaret Mead calls prefigurative learning.[11] In previous generations the young have always learned from the old. The information, history, values, myths, rituals—everything we have come to think of as culture—have been passed along from the elder to the younger. We now see a reverse of that situation. Today children still learn from adults, but adults learn even more from children. This means that there will eventually be more equal transactions between adults and children, more genuine exchanges of values and information. Under these circumstances the possibilities for indoctrination are greatly reduced.[12]

Indoctrination will also be minimized when parents and teachers become less powerful, when education becomes voluntary instead of compulsory, and when children are given their rights in all our institutions. If education is truly self-determined, then the child has a better chance to grow into maturity having developed his values on the basis of personal experience rather than as a result of adult indoctrination.

The enormous apparatus of American education has withstood the efforts of educational reformers because their work was based on an expectation that both educators and society wanted it to change, to be more humane. They were wrong in that expectation. Educators are not going to change education, nor is the society that is profiting from it. It can only change as a result of action from those who are exploited and oppressed by it—the children. The hope for the abolition of compulsory education and the reform of the educational establishment lies in the achievement of children's rights, specifically the right to educate oneself.

8

The Right to Freedom from Physical Punishment

In a curious paradox, Americans are becoming alarmed at the statistics relating to the battering and torturing of children, yet these same people overwhelmingly endorse a form of physical abuse of children that is far more common, and in a way even more of an assault on a child's dignity, a practice that is not only not illegal, but actually prescribed and protected by law. This is the humiliating practice of corporal punishment. The term "corporal punishment" means any bodily pain inflicted for the purpose of punishment, including the impulsive striking and roughing-up of children as well as the more ritualized and deliberate child beatings administered by a parent or a school official. Sociologist John Seeley offers a more precise definition:

> . . . the intentional, unplayful, deliberated infliction of physical pain on a person, because of his "wrongdoing," by a person claiming some standing other than that of the person harmed, by at least [a] partial consent of the victim, somewhat ceremonialized, amounting to less than "torture," and intended to hurt without harming.[1]

Corporal punishment has been practiced since the beginning of recorded history. One finds a number of Biblical passages advocating its use: "Foolishness is bound up in the heart of the child but the rod of correction shall drive it far from him." (Proverbs 22:15.) "Withhold not correction from the child, for if thou beatest him with the rod he shall not die. Thou shalt beat him with a rod and deliver his soul from hell." (Proverbs 23:13,14.) Moses insisted upon even harsher penalties when he commanded, "If a man has a stubborn and rebellious son which will not obey the voice of his mother, and that when they have chastened him will not harken unto them, then shall his father and his mother lay hold of him, and bring him out unto the gate of his place. . . . and all the men of the city shall stone him with stones that he die . . ." (Deuteronomy 21:18.) The remarkable difference between the Old and the New Testament in the way in which people are encouraged to treat children led one little girl to remark that God must have written the Old Testament before He became a Christian.

Corporal punishment has been common law for centuries. Its use is so well accepted and widespread that it is difficult to find a society which does not resort to its application in some form. It is used impulsively in the home, deliberately in the schools, and sadistically in the penal institutions for children. No one knows how pervasive the practice is within the family, but estimates of its use in the public school system in American run into tens of thousands and probably into hundreds of thousands of cases annually. In one medium-sized city, Dallas, Texas, there were, during a nine-month period in 1971, 5,358 reported spankings, and many go unreported. A teacher in the Belman School in Pittsburgh claims that there were ten to twenty spankings administered every day.

School children are grabbed, pulled, pushed, choked, thrown against walls and knocked unconscious. Earrings are pulled off their pierced ears, chairs are jerked out from under them, their mouths are stuffed with paper. They are beaten with all kinds of weapons including sticks, straps, belts, shoes, pine boards, fists, paddles of all shapes and sizes, modified baseball bats, canes, TV antennas. All this punishment for crimes such as mistakes in homework, not beeing dressed properly in gym classes, failure to pay towel fees, tardiness, fighting, misspelling words, sailing paper airplanes, mumbling, inattentiveness, possessing bubble gum or potato chips, failure to say "Sir," talking without permission, insolence, having one's shirttails out, missing the waste paper basket, talking back, smoking, truancy, putting one's feet on the desk, covering a book, cursing—in short, whatever exasperates or frustrates a teacher or administrator, and particularly those behaviors which flout or challenge authority.

The vast majority of students are not physically harmed by corporal punishment, but there are assaults which produce welts, bruises, cuts, hemorrhaging and some injuries requiring hospitalization. Corporal punishment is used repeatedly, unevenly, arbitrarily and often sadistically. Its use is heaviest with emotionally disturbed children and children from minority groups.

As unwarranted, irrational, and cruel as it may seem, corporal punishment has yet to become a national disgrace. Quite to the contrary, it is one of the most commonly accepted and heartily endorsed methods of discipline in our country. Gallup polls indicate that 62 percent of all Americans favor the use of corporal punishment, while only 2 percent think that the discipline in public schools is too strict. This same group cites the lack of discipline as the number one problem in our schools.[2]

It is not only the general public that favors the use of physical violence to bring about conformity. In 1969 the National Education Association surveyed its membership of professional educators, finding that 65 percent of the elementary educators and 55 percent of the secondary educators favored "judicious use of violent bodily punishment." In Pittsburg, 70 percent of the teachers signed a petition asking for a ban on spanking to be lifted.[3]

Corporal punishment is not only sanctioned by common law but is prescribed by legislation in almost every state in the United States. Only three states now have laws against the use of corporal punishment: Massachusetts, New Jersey, and Maryland. And in Maryland a number of counties have acted to reinstate its use. It has been banned in several cities: Washington (D.C.), New York City, Pittsburg, Baltimore, Chicago, Grosse Pointe (Michigan) and in some individual school districts. There are many places where it is not used. For example, most European countries have banned it—London, just recently.

While in a number of places strenuous efforts are being made to eliminate corporal punishment, most of the recent legislation and court decisions tend to favor it. A recent action by the U.S. Supreme Court let stand a lower court ruling which permitted the Dallas school system to continue corporal punishment. Eight states have newly adopted legislation which encourages its use. Regardless of preventive measures taken, it is still employed unofficially —even in those cities which have made its use illegal—and officially in almost all public schools.

Actually it is legal almost everywhere, employed in about 80 percent of the school districts and relied upon heavily in about 20 percent.

The American Civil Liberties Union in a treatise prepared by Allen Reitman, Judith Follman, and Edward Ladd has opposed the use of force in controlling students by attacking what it regards to be the violation of the constitutional rights of students. Arguing first of all that there is no age limit on the protection which the Constitution affords, the ACLU goes on to question the concept, *in loco parentis,* which is the justification most frequently used in the abrogation of students' rights. This Latin term, literally translated "in place of the parent," has gradually come to mean that certain institutions, notably schools, can act in a parental capacity in the absence of the child's natural parents, and therefore have the right to exert certain measures of force, including corporal punishment, to which they might not otherwise be entitled. The concept *in loco parentis* was first used by the famous British jurist, Blackstone, to protect individual tutors and governesses in the employ of a household so that they might operate in a disciplinary fashion similar to that of the parents. Today this concept has been extended to institutions and to the hundred or more teachers and administrators whom the student might encounter during his lifetime in school. Moreover, it no longer necessarily reflects the wishes of the individual parent. Parents may indicate to school administrators that they do not desire the use of corporal punishment for their children and yet the school authorities can and do continue to use this punishment against the child and remain within the law. Clearly, the *in loco parentis* doctrine no longer applies according to its original intent.

A more serious flaw in the application of this doctrine is the implication that the school has the right to beat children because parents have that right. It is this assumption which must be challenged if dignity and respect are ever to be fully extended to children. No parent, let alone a school official, should have the right to beat his children.

The constitutionality of corporal punishment in the schools is also challenged on the basis that it violates one's rights to due process of the law. Even though the Supreme Court has made it clear in the Tinker decision that the schools cannot have absolute control and authority over persons, in school or out (in this instance control meant the denial of student's right to wear black armbands as a protest against war), the student still operates in a closed system where most consitutional guarantees simply do not apply. Due process ordinarily means that a person will be told of the charges against him, given the right to counsel, the opportunity to rebut the charges in a fair hearing, and perhaps most importantly, the accuser, the judge and the executioner will not be the same person. This is seldom the case in the administration of corporal punishment in the schools today. Because schools are government institutions, corporal punishment in the schools is therefore equivalent to a government act and should be particularly subject to the restraints of the Constitution.

Corporal punishment is also opposed on constitutional grounds as evidence of cruel and unusual punishment. Cruel and unusual, because it applies only to children. The use of physical violence has been eliminated from our attempts to correct the behavior of adults. No adult prisons officially condone the use of physical violence. It is even illegal to use such force against animals. Yet, ironically, it is legally applied in the most cruel and abusive ways to children. While corporal punishment cannot be used against convicted felons who may have committed rape, robbery, and murder, it is permitted against children.

Opponents of corporal punishment in the schools are apparently uneasy about challenging the practice on constitutional grounds alone. They seem to feel it necessary to augment their case by citing evidence that (1) the effects of corporal punishment on controlling behavior are short-term, inefficient, and often achieve just the opposite of what is intended; (2) schools using corporal punishment have more behavior problems than schools which do not; (3) there are negative consequences, not only for the student, but for the whole class who must witness the violence and live with the threat of it; (4) children who are repeatedly punished remain frequent offenders; (5) rather than using corporal punishment as a last resort, it is often used impulsively upon first provocation; (6) children who are beaten are often those who are in treatment for emotional disturbance; (7) corporal punishment is often used against aggressive children, lower class children, and minority group children because "that is the only language they understand." Moreover, opponents of corporal punishment suggest that those who use it demonstrate a pathetic lack of knowledge and a poverty of ideas about what to do, pointing out the existence of many more acceptable alternatives for controlling behavior extant in modern psychology, deriving mainly from the theories of behavior modification developed by B. F. Skinner and his associates. The argument that corporal punishment is ineffective and unnecessary seems to imply that if corporal punishment really did work then it might be all right to use it; if it were used only as a last resort then it might be legitimate; if it could be used "fairly" then it might be an acceptable means of behavior control.

The real issue, however, is that corporal punishment violates children's rights. It deprives the child of the right to life, liberty, and property without due process of law. It cannot be condoned under any circumstances, even if it did "work." For this reason alone, it must be eliminated from the arsenal of weapons used against children to force their compliance and submission to authority.

Harried parents may still ask, "If I can't resort to corporal punishment, what *can* I do to control my children?" A natural question, to which almost any child specialist will have a dozen answers, each explaining a thoughtful and gentle way to control children. They are quick to provide such answers because, first of all, they have the time to think about creative responses to children, but also because they, and almost everyone else never question the fundamental *right* of the parent to control the behavior of the child. One might even say that the parent has the *duty* to control the child, all the time, everywhere.

Society pities parents who cannot control their children, judging them to be weak, insecure, guilty, and negligent. The first requirement of parenthood is to be able to gain control of the child. For those parents who are unable to do so by ordering, persuading, reasoning, and other less punitive methods, most people feel it is entirely justifiable to resort to corporal punishment, because winning the battle is clearly the most important concern.

That parents should establish total and complete authority over their children is such an accepted part of our child psychology, so fundamental to almost everything else that is said about the relationship of parent and child, that it is indeed difficult to see beyond it. Someday the control of children by parents may not be the most important aspect of the relationship, just as the control of a woman by a man is no longer the most important aspect of that relationship. Some day we may see that it is neither possible nor desirable to control children, to win every battle. We will see that there is another way to be with children in which the power of the parent is limited by his respect for a child's rights, in which there is mutual influence, give and take, and the problems are not resolved on a win-lose basis.[4]

Controlling the behavior of children seems to be important to parents for at least four reasons:

The first reason certainly must be that they believe that parental control is good for their children; that children associate control with caring and love, that children need the parent to be the rulemaker, that without control children cannot be made to learn what they must know.

The second reason for exerting behavior control is that without it, a parent's life would be terribly difficult—maybe impossible. Parents are burdened with the complex task of living with children who, because of their limited circumstances, demand such constant attention and supervision that control is needed most of the time. Time when parents can share thoughts and feelings with their children and explore new dimensions of their lives together is highly limited, compared with the time spent in making sure that children behave themselves.

The third reason for controlling children's behavior is that children are seen as products of the parents and must reflect well on them. Parents need to be proud of their offspring. The behavior and appearance of their children is part of the parents' image. Understandably they want it to be a good one. Men have long believed that their wives should complement their personal images, and while we may be moving away from that idea somewhat, we still maintain it fully with respect to children. The idea that a child might be regarded as an autonomous person with a separate identity is foreign enough, but to suggest that he should have the right to be ill-tempered or unattractive is all but impossible to accept. While it embarrasses us when adults in our families don't behave the way we wish they would, we do respect their right to be themselves. So far we have not learned to respect the same right for children.

The fourth need for behavior control is to make certain that the child will respond immediately and automatically to the parents' command in the case of an emergency where the child risks injury or death. Without immediate obedience to such commands as, "Stop!" or "Don't drink that," parents feel that they would not be able to protect the child from danger. We have borrowed the concept of automatic obedience from the military, where it is used for just the opposite reasons—to send people into dangerous situations. Parents increasingly rely on such discipline as the world becomes a more dangerous place for children. In examining what the emergency situations are that require such obedience, more often than not they are man-made dangers which, with proper design, could be made safe for children. The instant obedience of children is seldom necessary with respect to natural dangers such as trees and cliffs, but it is absolutely vital when it comes to the dangers of a speeding automobile, poison under the sink, or a backyard swimming pool. Man-made dangers are different from natural dangers partly because natural dangers usually look dangerous, and so signal the child to be careful. Moreover, with natural dangers one usually has time to explain and teach, for one mistake would not ordinarily be fatal. Unfortunately, man has created many dangers for which one mistake is fatal to the child.

Do parents need complete authority and control over their children? Probably the importance of these factors to child rearing has been greatly over-estimated. In one sense it is impossible *not* to control children, just as we are continually controlling all people with whom we interact. In fact, we try hardest to control people we care most about. It is usually an act of love and we could not abandon its practice even if we tried. But to have one's parenting dominated by authority and control can hardly be translated as loving. Parents probably need exercise no more control than one adult does over another when he "does something for the other's good" or warns him of danger. Most other needs to control stem from ego problems or from situations which, with better design, could be avoided, such as the design of better living arrangements for families so that parents are less burdened, or the better design of man-made objects so that they are not dangerous for children. If we would place more of an emphasis on correcting the situations rather than correcting the children, we could rely less on authoritarian control. In any case corporal punishment is not appropriate to achieve such control.

Some state laws imply that corporal punishment ought not be used in anger, but in a dispassionate and deliberate form. Yet who can hit a child when there is no anger? Surely it is better to hit only in anger. These laws prescribe that corporal punishment is to be administered by someone remote from the child. Yet who would want someone who does not love the child to hit him? The situation is truly paradoxical.[5]

An argument exists that corporal punishment is maintained in schools and elsewhere because it is sexually gratifying. John Seeley suggests that corporal punishment is on both sides the enactment of a sexual drama, a thinly disguised expression of forbidden and deeply repressed sexual wishes. In a paper on the sexual overtones of corporal punishment he says:

> It is not, of course, being asserted that every formal corporal punishment is but a "barely disguised homosexual assault" . . . It is being maintained that all such punishments by public authority, particularly in penal institutions, furnish objectively point-for-point and element-for-element correspondences, and, for many, open the way to all-but-conscious gratification of the forbidden impulses. Consider as

> correspondences only the forced partial or total undressing of the victim, against protest; the bodily site of the punishment; the early struggle and the hopeless submission; the implement, phallic in form; the movement so constrained physically that only pelvic thrusts and gluteal contraction are possible; the cries of increasing helplessness . . . What more? [6]

The question of whether or not corporal punishment gives sexual gratification is one that can only be known subjectively. But there are consequences of corporal punishment, extremely serious ones, which can be understood objectively. They have to do with the circularity of aggression. The more that aggression is met with aggression, the more the problem is escalated. The most tragic consequence of corporal punishment is that it breeds violence. David Gil, in his book *Violence Against Children* points out that it is our acceptance and legitimization of violence—particularly corporal punishment—which encourages, and in fact produces, more serious abuses of children.[7]

When compulsory education ends, corporal punishment in schools will end. Schools are the last remaining institutions that officially condone its use. If teachers did not have to act like jailers, if students were free to commit themselves to the learning experience or to leave, then the need to control behavior, to worry constantly about problems of discipline, would be greatly reduced and perhaps even eliminated. We can have a less violent school system when we make it voluntary.

Physical punishment is not the worst that we do to children. Violence done to their spirits is worse. Our actions which make them feel guilty and stupid and impotent are probably far more destructive in the long run. Noninjurious physical punishment has at least the positive value of being clear and understandable, however degrading and inhumane it may be. We cannot always protect children against abuses to their spirit, just as we cannot protect ourselves. It is possible, however, for us to end the use of corporal punishment in the schools and even in the home. This can happen only if we come to recognize that bodily violence is a crime against children, a violation of their rights. It does not belong in our repertoire of responses to children.

9

The Right to Sexual Freedom

When the subject of sexual freedom for children arises, as it invariably does in any serious discussion of children's rights, the temptation is to avoid it altogether. One risks losing people who might otherwise be sympathetic to the liberation of children. The subject of sex, even adult sex, is so charged with emotion, so hopelessly clouded by hypocrisy, superstition, and myth, so curiously attached to seemingly unrelated issues—such as respect for authority, rock music, and the communist conspiracy—that there is little chance that arguments in the area of sex will be as coolly judged as those in other areas. Nevertheless, the temptation to bypass the subject must be overcome. Not only because it is a fundamental issue and is sure to be on the minds of the readers, but because, as Bertrand Russell, Paul Goodman, and many others have pointed out, we are guilty of harmful cowardice when we fail to deal forthrightly with the subject of child sex.

The sexual revolution of the sixties has often been dismissed, even maligned, as having been more talk than action. Adults who know that sexual attitudes have changed considerably sometimes seem a bit disappointed to learn that sexual behavior, even among the young, has not changed all that much. Sexual behavior, of course, has never matched sexual attitudes, but now, at least among the young, the attitudes are more liberal than the behavior. In past generations it was the other way around. In any case we are partially indebted to this revolution for creating the climate which makes this discussion at all possible.

The first aspect of the child's right to sexual freedom is his right to information about sex. The term information rather than education is used to separate the child's right to know, to be able to obtain facts, to have questions answered, and to have access to any information available to any adults, from the responsibility that an institution would have in teaching children about sex. The availability of information is surely important, but whether we should have sex education in the schools as they are presently structured needs to be reconsidered. In a monolithic system of compulsory public education, a student learns about sex in an atmosphere that is compromised, sterile, uninspired, passionless, clinical, nuclear family-oriented, leering, sexist, and value-laden, one in which sex must be linked with love, maturity, and marriage. It is likely to be taught by instructors who believe that they are teaching the formal curriculum when in fact they are teaching their underlying attitudes which are almost certain to reflect middle class values of the importance of postponement, moderation, marriage, and heterosexuality. This is the situation if one is lucky. In the unlucky situation, sex education is so full of myth and superstition, embarrassment and frustration, guilt and shame, that the subject is better left completely out of the curriculum.

While it is desirable for many institutions and agencies, including schools, to make useful sex information available to children, it may be unwise to give the major burden of sex education to the public schools as we now do. There, vast numbers of unqualified teachers are asked to give a standardized course based on what the administrators of twenty-six thousand school districts can agree on as acceptable for children. Courses offering more than watered-down treatments of reproductive biology or a Walt Disney version of sex education quickly become so controversial that the teacher is incapacitated and vulnerable to loss of employment. What is actually learned by everyone is just how hot a subject sex is. Teachers in most schools have a difficult enough time teaching the traditional subjects for which there is enthusiastic community support, why make their situation even worse by asking them to take on the additional responsibility of teaching sex education? If there is one subject that should not be taught badly, it is sex.

The irony is that sex education is treated as if adults actually knew about sex and children didn't, which of course is not true. Children don't know more than adults, but the ignorance of adults is monumental. But then how could adults have learned? Having performed sex acts hardly provides the necessary information to inform others about sex, any more than having been sick enables one to be a doctor. The persistence of misinformation is truly incredible. In a study of five Philadelphia medical schools in 1959, half of the graduating doctors and 20 percent of the faculty still believed that masturbation led to mental illness.[1] Such findings make one wonder to whom we can turn for sex information.

Turning to the school system has given us sex information dominated by what Mary Breasted has called "the worship of normalcy."[2] The requirement that the sexuality of single people be ignored, that sex be taught as a part of education for family life, limited to the heterosexual activities of a married couple and emphasizing its procreative functions, has led to an even greater pressure to conform to the traditional goal of self-fulfillment through the creation of a nuclear family.

Few teachers understand how strong that pressure is and how easily and unconsciously they exert it. In many elementary schools, children who do not live in nuclear families are in the majority. Yet the amount of pressure to appear "normal" is so great, that when asked to draw their families, these children will actually fake a family with mother and father and several children. Teachers can communicate this worship of normalcy simply by asking a child what his or her father's name is. Many children who have no live-in father simply don't know. This assumption of the desirability and universality of nuclear family life dominates all sex education programs and presents major barriers to the presentation of material on premarital sex (even the term loads the question), on homosexuality, and on the many variations and pleasures of both child and adult sexuality.

Surely there can be more and better sex education programs available to children in schools and elsewhere, but (1) we cannot expect schools to do the entire job, (2) the broad and varied range of human sexuality should be included, which means that instructors would be responsible for a great deal of personal and professional development and the continued acquisition of new knowledge, (3) in addition to special courses, sex education should be fused with learning about literature, history, art, science, society, and with all of the life situations in which it has meaning and importance.

While it may not be possible or desirable to completely demystify sex—not that we need to worry much about that ever happening—it is possible to remove many of the present barriers to a child's finding out about sex. The first step is to realize that sexual attitudes are taught mainly by indirect methods. Moving a child's hands away from his genitals, changing the subject when it appears that the conversation might enter sexual territory, maintaining a shroud of secrecy over the whole business is, in itself, sex education. Manufacturing children's dolls which have no genitalia teaches the child that adults do not want him to look at, touch, or think about genitalia or their functions. These attitudes and distortions are the major and inescapable lessons which our society offers and progress in sex education will always be limited, at least to some extent, by the prevalence of such attitudes and distortions.

The first and most difficult job, then, is to relax our own attitudes about sex and raise our consciousness on the entire subject. In so doing, adults may get better at giving children answers to questions about sex even when the questions are not asked. Most questions now receive mythical or simplistic answers, more to protect the parent than the child. The right to sex information implies the right to a straightforward answer from a parent or teacher. Contrary to the usual advice, a lengthy and technical explanation is often exactly what is needed to answer a child's simple questions; the child-rearing books that caution parents to "keep it simple" may really be responding more to parents' needs, knowing how much they want to be let off the hook on these matters, than to the children's. Such advice also reflects some of the myth of childhood in underscoring our idea that children are not ready for straightforward talk.

Secondly, the right to sex information would mean eliminating all forms of censorship which keep children ignorant about sex and giving them access to all of the information to which adults have access. Specifically, this would include books in libraries which, as we have seen, are arbitrarily and systematically kept out of the hands of children. Much to the discomfort of adults, it would also include the right to enter stores and theaters where "adults only" films, magazines, and other sexual entertainment is presented. Pornography is neither one of the best nor one of the most common sources of sex information, but we must recognize it as an important source, even if we find it personally distasteful. Although the pictures of sex which one receives from pornography are at least as distorted as those from public school sex education, they can provide many answers which the child simply does not get from adults.

No one has yet determined whether or not such material is harmful to either adults or children, or whether or not it precipitates sex crimes. The question of whether or not pornography is harmful is, again, beside the point. If it is information available to adults, it must also be available to children.

Even if we wanted to eliminate pornography, there is probably no way to do it. Certainly there would be no way of eliminating all the material that people find sexually stimulating. In the examination of sex offenders and child molesters it has been found that one of the most sexually exciting pictures to them is the widely displayed advertisement for Coppertone Suntan Lotion, which shows a small black dog tugging at the bathing suit of a little blonde girl and exposing her bare bottom. It is absurd to try to eliminate such material. Some people even find the telephone book to be sexually stimulating!

The right to sex information would also include the right to information about birth control and venereal disease. Such information, without access to the necessary drugs, equipment, and materials is, of course, useless. Along with better information, there must be ways of providing children with the contraceptive and protective devices and materials that are suitable for them.

The situation is now truly absurd. Our insanity is evident when we give people information about birth control pills, but not the pills themselves. We teach boys how to protect themselves from venereal disease, but they cannot legally purchase the condoms necessary to provide such protection. It has been the policy in some institutions to give a girl birth control information only *after* she has become pregnant.

Our problem has been that we have tried to manage, filter, and block the flow of sex information; as a result we are constantly embarrassed by ridiculous inconsistencies. If all of the restrictions on sex-information were lifted, censorship and management would not be necessary, and the consequent insanities could be avoided.

The worry is that sex education will lead to "premature" sexuality and therefore to traumatic emotional problems. We seem oblivious to the fact that other educational experiences, imposed on children without hesitation, frequently and predictably lead to emotional traumas. Compulsory education is terribly difficult for many children. Final exams can be as traumatic as any adult calamity, as the suicide rate at American universities during final exam week will demonstrate. If what we want to do is reduce the amount of emotional stress people experience—and surely we don't want to live in a world without emotional stress—there are many more significant changes we could make than eliminating the discussion of sex.

All education can be dangerous. It is probably the most dangerous of human enterprises, constantly threatening us with change. Our belief that opening all the doors of knowledge will ultimately improve mankind and lead to social progress is still unproven. But we can be sure that its opposite, the suppression of knowledge, has given man his darkest times.

Another major element in sexual freedom for children is to avoid the conditioning which presently shapes boys and girls into the stereotyped roles of men and women. From the moment a pink blanket is wrapped around a little girl and a blue one around a little boy, society treats them differently.

The conditioning to which the little girl is subjected trains her to believe that she should be delicate, graceful, and passive. As she grows older she learns that she shouldn't be too rough, too independent, too tomboyish, too intelligent, or too good at math and science. She shouldn't be faster, smarter, taller, or stronger than boys; as a matter of fact she should learn to accept her dependence on them. As she enters maturity she should look for fulfillment in being sought after, finding and attracting a man, marrying him, having his children, emotionally supporting him, making a good home, being a good mother, and if she is lucky, she will reach the crowning achievement of having orgasms. Women are raised to be receptive, nurturing, aesthetic, emotional, irrational, gentle, understanding, tender, comforting, childlike, virtuous, innocent—in short, "feminine."

Boys are similarly trapped into roles that don't necessarily fit their desires, abilities, or basic characteristics. We expect boys to be aggreessive, brave, and rough and tumble. They are expected to get dirty, play rough, extend themselves, breathe hard, and sweat. As boys become men they are expected to excel both intellectually and athletically, to be good providers, to be able to fix things and make things, hunt and fish and fight. Men should be where the action is, making money, making decisions, making things happen, amounting to something, becoming somebody. Men should be more interested in things than in people, and when they deal with people they must be able to take charge, to dominate everyone—particularly women and children and all those who are subordinates. A man's physical prowess should be matched only by his sexual prowess. Masculinity is being rugged, tough, independent, individualistic, assertive, rational, virile, potent, decisive, strong, and courageous. John Wayne. Ernest Hemingway.

The little girl is never expected to be anybody in her own right. She will have what sociologists call relational identity, that is, she receives her identity through others, the men in her life. She is somebody's daughter, then somebody's wife, then somebody's mother, but never somebody. Even if she becomes somebody, she still must validate herself through her ability to function as a wife and a mother. When the newspapers report on the achievements of a woman judge, which is quite rare in itself, it is always necessary to make clear that, in addition to her professional life, she is a happy wife and mother. Articles about men rarely include such information.

Men's roles, and women's also, have for too long been shaped by a locker-room mentality in which men are judged by their sexual conquests and their "machismo," while women are judged by their beauty and popularity. Among some young people in college these rigid stereotypes are relaxing, as evidenced by the declining status of the football player and homecoming queen and the broader definitions of what a young person might be and do to gain status with his or her peers. But by and large, the traditional stereotypes remain dominant in American culture.

One of the most pervasive and yet most disabling concepts in modern psychology is the belief that people need sex role identity. The concept of sexual identity has been so persuasively argued by Freud, Erikson, and many others that it is indeed difficult to question. We seem to be totally convinced that little boys need fathers and little girls need mothers, or at least that they need around them adults of the same sex with whom to identify. Without these models the child would not know who he or she is and would grow up unhealthy, confused, and afraid.

The well-accepted view that every child should have a strong father and a soft mother has struck fear into the hearts of the seven million single mothers in the United States who raise their children alone. Worried and guilty, they fear that their little boys won't grow up knowing what a man is. Society pities the poor mother who tells horror stories of her little boy sitting down to urinate or borrowing her razor and pretending to shave his legs. These stories frighten us and we can't help but believe that, yes, the boy certainly does need a man around the house. The pressure on the mother to find one is great indeed.

Worrying about such matters is the real trouble.

It is crippling the entire society. Do we really want our little boys and girls to continue to grow up in these stereotypical ways that adults know are terrible traps? The heavy pressures to conform to these roles, the lack of any opportunity to escape them, the absence of consciousness of what it's like to be a man or a woman, these are the matters we should be concerned about. Instead the formal and informal sexist training continues and leads all children into these debilitating and oppressive sex roles.

The fear is that children will not be able to live up to the stereotypes: that boys will be nonathletic, passive, delicate, impotent, or worst of all, homosexual; that girls will be roughneck, homely, assertive and perhaps worst of all, lesbian. No, perhaps the most terrible epithet that can be hurled at a woman is that she is an aggressive, castrating bitch. This, of course, translates into the accusation that she is simply acting like a man. To guarantee sex role conditioning, children's books illustrate boys doing all the interesting things and girls helping them. The boys are usually taller. They are at least four times, perhaps as much as fifteen times, as likely to be shown doing something physically active or creative. Nursery schools, kindergartens—and the entire school system, for that matter—continue the sexual distinctions both in play activity (the boys doing more vigorous things, the girls preparing to be homemakers) and in organizational structure (women teachers with men as their leaders).

We may have greatly overestimated the differences between males and females. There are obvious biological differences: men impregnate; women menstruate, conceive and lactate, but there may not be too many other differences that are not culturally learned. Children's bodies are different only in genitalia. Girls behave differently from boys mainly because of social learning.

We may be unnecessarily stressing sex differences. Margaret Mead has argued for years that there are greater differences within a sex than between the sexes. Even if there are differences between sexes, are they ones we want to perpetuate, are they ones around which we would want to build a society? We must draw a fine line between respecting differences and discriminating against people on the basis of those differences. In most cases we would not want to use these differences as the basis for designing our institutions or our educational programs.

Children need freedom from narrow and constricting roles if they are to enjoy their full sexuality as human beings. If we remain so intent on perpetuating stereotypes, we will be depriving children, in the most fundamental way, of the right to sexual freedom.

For the most part, informed people are prepared to accept the child's right to sex information and his or her right to non-sexist child rearing, but the right to engage freely in sexual activity puts even the most ardent child liberator through some difficult tests.

Most sex educators, if not most Americans, now pride themselves on their enlightened attitude toward masturbation, admitting that it doesn't cause insanity or other physical damage to a person. But there is always the wish that the child wouldn't spend so much time doing it. Even one of the most permissive of our child-rearing specialists, Haim Ginott, says, "Parents may exert mild pressure against self-indulgence, not because it is pathological, but because it is not progressive; it does not result in social relationships or personal growth."[3] Dr. Spock, in an otherwise highly permissive statement about masturbation says, "Even if we could magically get over our disapproval (which I don't think would be desirable), the fact would remain that our child lives in and must adapt to a society that disapproves. Furthermore, there is lots of evidence that all children feel guilty about masturbation whether or not their parents have found out about it, or said anything about it. So I think it quite appropriate that when a mother discovers a child in sex play to give him the idea that she doesn't want him to do it any more, in a tone that implies that this will help him to stop. With the child who needs reassurance the mother can explain that most boys and girls want to do it sometime or another but they can usually stop when they try."[4]

Not only are we left feeling that in spite of this reassurance there really may be something wrong with masturbation (other than the guilt that we attach to it), but the Masters and Johnson discovery is seldom mentioned: the most exciting sexual experiences come (1) from mechanical manipulations such as vibrators; (2) from activities of self-indulgence, such as masturbation; and (3) from coitus, or normal heterosexual intercourse in that order. Nor do we hear much about their findings that the earlier in life sexuality begins, the later in life it continues. Perhaps the main reason that masturbation is acceptable, at least to some degree, is the secret hope that it will postpone heterosexual activity for both boys and girls until they are old enough to avoid conception or contraction of venereal disease.

Masturbation is almost always associated with boys. Many girls do not even believe that the word applies to them. This is due to the age-old belief that girls simply do not have as much sexuality as boys and don't need to masturbate, but a great many young girls do, and there is some reason to believe that those who enjoy masturbation tend to experience a more successful adult sex life.

When children's sex play and mutual exploration in pairs or in groups takes place, the concern becomes greater. Most parents will tolerate small children playing doctor, pulling up skirts, or dropping pants, but as children get older, parental anxiety mounts until such behavior is forbidden and punished. Although ideally we may want to allow our children to fully explore and experience their own and each other's anatomies, as well as their feelings and sensations of sexuality, apprehension is an understandable reaction and perhaps not an altogether harmful one. What, for example, does a parent do when he opens the bedroom door and discovers his child engaged in some form of sex play with one or more of the neighbor's children: Is he to tell them to stop, get dressed and leave, or pretend that he didn't notice, or apologize for interrupting and tell them to go on and enjoy themselves? If he does the last, the neighbor's children may report his attitude to their parents and cause a rupture in all of the relationships between playmates and parents. This outcome could be more disturbing to the child than the customary suppression of sexual experience. Even observing children's rights does not provide parents with a clear idea of how to behave in such complex situations. This is an area in which no expert can give meaningful advice. Parents actions will depend entirely upon how embarrassed, angry, or desperate they feel. In all probability, one could find fault with whatever they do.

So far the discussion has dealt only with sexual activities that are generally considered normal for our culture. Crossing the line into the areas of sexual intercourse with age mates, pedophilia (adult-child sex), incest, and sexual molestation not only enters the dangerous territory of criminal behavior, but calls up the most deeply repressed fears and the most powerful taboos of our society. It is in these areas that advocates for children's sexual freedom risk the greatest amount of alienation. The Sexual

Freedom League is one organization which advocates sex between children but not pedophilia or incest. Its policy statement makes a commitment to childhood sexuality, freedom from repression, and the acceptability of intercourse even among children. They give the example of intercourse between a twelve-year-old boy and a ten-year-old girl. There are, of course, cultures in which intercourse at this age is not at all uncommon, and there are even subcultures within our society where it exists.[5]

Even if the idea of sexual intercourse between children is acceptable, the idea of sexual freedom between adults and children is so disturbing that it appalls practically everybody who might otherwise support sexual freedom for children. Pedophilia, child molestation, and incest are all subjects which conjure up the most horrifying images. Nothing —including murder and rape—is more heavily tabooed or more severely penalized than adult-child sex. In some states the maximum sentence is fifty years, in others, life imprisonment.[6]

Almost everyone has difficulty accepting the fact that children are not only sensual but sexual, and that some are capable of sexual activity almost from birth.[7] Kinsey reports that "Full display of physiologic changes which are typical of the response of an adult have been observed in both female and male infants as young as four months of age."[8] Another myth is that adult-child sex usually forces physical violence and sexual activity on an unwilling child.[9] That is not usually true. In many instances, the child is a willing participant. One must be careful not to assume that such willingness is necessarily genuine consent. It may be engineered consent, by promise, seduction, or coercion. But engineered consent is not only a problem for children. Adults have an identical problem in understanding the issue of consent, particularly when it relates to investigations of rape, in which it is very difficult to prove violation without consent. Seduction, coercion, indoctrination, whatever is used to engineer consent, is wrong at all ages, not just for children.

What children really need is the option to refuse. The freedom not to engage in sexual activity is as important as any other aspect of sexual freedom. But children are raised in such a way that they cannot refuse adults. Parents have insisted that children accept all forms of affection from relatives and friends—being picked up, fondled, hugged, kissed, pinched, tickled, squeezed—leaving children with little experience in saying no. They also have little experience in trusting their own reactions to people and in resisting the promise of rewards. They are not informed about sexual matters, do not understand their own sexuality or that of others, and thus cannot cope effectively in this area. We keep children ignorant and then worry that they are vulnerable to sexual advances.

The most ruinous situations are usually not the sexual activities involved in the act of molestation, but the community's response to the act when it has been discovered. The guilt and the fear that are induced can be worse than the experience of the act itself.

It is impossible to treat the terrible violence and grotesque actions of some child molestations casually. One can only be horrified by the actions that some adults take against children. But our horror over these rare instances and our strong taboo about adult-child sex has led to the application of the most severe penalties to even the most innocent acts of affection. The penalty is not appropriate to the crime and probably neither cures nor deters. We can and should decriminalize sexual relations between consenting people. Assault and kidnapping laws already on the books would cover the cases which involve force, abduction, or abuse. The remaining cases are better dealt with by improved sex education, enlightened sexual attitudes, and an increased respect for children's rights.

Incest and sexual activity within the family, whether it be father-daughter, mother-son, brother-sister or any homosexual combination of those partners, is far more common and far less traumatic than we have always been led to believe. Perhaps no activity is more tabooed in our society, yet current estimates of the number of Americans who have been involved in incestuous experience run as high as twenty million; that is, one in every ten people.[10] Studies of incest reveal that the dangers have been highly overrated. Christopher Bagley of the Institute of Psychiatry in London writes:

> A number of conclusions emerge from the review of reports of incest behavior. First, there is abundant evidence that from a young age the child has sexual desires and aspirations. When presented with the opportunity of a sexual relation with the opposite sexed parent, the child enters this relation not unwillingly, and may participate in it over a period of years. There does not appear to be any natural revulsion to incest in the child; indeed, the opposite sex parent seems to be a covert but significant figure in his sexual life. In the usual course of development, this sexual relationship becomes strongly tabooed as the child's age increases, and a process of "repression" ensues by which the child's relationship with the opposite sexed parent becomes explicity non-sexual."[11]

Sometimes incest occurs because it become functional to the preservation of the family, for example, if the wife is an invalid. When a family member, as Bagley puts it, "is socialized in the norms of incest, whether it is seen by the family to be functional for the survival of the family or because it is desired for some other reason by some dominant family members, the evidence from case histories shows that incest can be accepted by the younger partner with equanimity."[12] A number of writers, including Karl Menninger and Germaine Greer, have argued that incest itself does not usually produce detrimental effects on the child. Menninger, in his 1942 book, *Love Against Hate,* said:

> The assumption is, of course, that children are irreparably ruined by such experiences. Without intending in the least to justify or excuse such criminal behavior I may nevertheless point out that in the cold light of scientific investigation no such devastating effects usually follow (a fact which I hope will be of some comfort to certain anguished parents). Two psychiatrists (Lauretta Bender and Abram Blau) recently made a careful follow-up study of such cases and concluded that children exposed to premature sexual experiences with adults frequently turn out to be "distinguished and unusually charming and attractive in their outward personalities."
>
> The conclusion to be drawn from such observations need not be shocking; they simply bear out our contention that sexuality is not the evil and horrible thing it is generally conceived to be. Such experiences are traumatic to the child only when connected with deep hostilities; the furtive and desperate nature of such attacks, combined with the attitude of society toward them, tends entirely in the direction of unbearably stimulating the child's hostilities so that he conceives of sex as brutality. But when the experience actually stimulates the child erotically, it would appear from the observations

> of the authors cited just above that it may favor rather than inhibit the development of social capabilities and mental health in the so-called victims.[13]

Germaine Greer describes the situation of a friend:

> One woman I know enjoyed sex with an uncle all through her childhood, and never realized that anything unusual was toward until she went away to school. What disturbed her then was not what her uncle had done but the attitude of her teachers and the school psychiatrist. They assumed that she must have been traumatized and disgusted and therefore in need of very special help. In order to capitulate to their expectations, she began to fake symptoms that she did not feel, until at length she began to feel truly guilty about not having been guilty. She ended up judging herself very harshly for this innate lechery.[14]

One interesting feature of the investigations of incest behavior is how careful children are to keep the secret and protect the parents. This apparently comes from some understanding of the importance of such confidences and not as a result of threats of retaliation. Children seem to have a complete understanding of what can and cannot be said and done without getting their parents in trouble.

Public anxiety about child molestation has deprived children of many dimensions of nonsexual intimacy with adults. Playground instructors who want to respond to children with physical closeness are prevented from doing so by policy and sometimes by law. They must never touch the children, give them first aid in the privacy of the medical facility, pick up or fondle a crying child. In Southern California where concern for illicit contact runs high, male teachers have been fired simply because little girls may have leaned up against them. Once the accusation of child molestation is made, it is virtually impossible to defend against it in any way that will protect one's job or reputation.

It is not easy to change society's attitudes about child sexuality, but it is possible to begin to decriminalize sexual behavior, to remove sex from the law books. In almost every respect, Scandinavia and Great Britain are ahead of the United States in the treatment of sexuality and sex crimes. The fact that our sexual laws would not be at all appropriate in many other cultures should motivate us to change our laws. These laws do not even reflect our own common behaviors or attitudes. To apply the most extreme penalties to the vast majority of cases involving adult-child sex is totally inappropriate. With all the variations of sexual behavior found around the world and throughout history, it is ridiculous to limit by law the ways in which people should be together sexually. The child's right to sexual freedom does not mean the advocacy of any particular form of sexuality for adults and children. What it does advocate is the freedom for children to conduct their own sexual lives with no more restrictions than adults. Further, that all sex activity be decriminalized so that sexual experimentation and sexual acts between consenting people can be enjoyed without fear of punishment.

If all this sounds too open and free, we must recognize that in this society—when it comes to matters of sexuality—we are not likely to err in the direction of too much freedom.

10

The Right to Economic Power

Money is power. It's not easy to start an argument with most Americans on that statement. Almost everyone agrees that money and power just seem to go together. For that reason the attempt to strengthen the rights of children without giving them access to economic power would surely be a futile exercise.

Economic power would give children the right to work, to acquire and manage money, to receive equal pay for equal work, to gain promotions to leadership positions, to own property, to develop a credit record, to enter into binding contracts, to engage in enterprise, to obtain guaranteed support apart from the family, and to achieve financial independence.

A more disturbing idea is difficult to imagine.

Not even the prospect of children exercising voting rights or enjoying sexual freedom is as troubling to many as is the prospect of the child demanding the right to financial power. Such a concept is so foreign to us and economic discrimination against children so deeply rooted that an effort to give children an economic power base is bound to meet with strong resistance—for understandable reasons. Extending these rights to children threatens our entire system, our way of life. Among other things, by making it possible for children to be financially independent, we relinquish many of the ways we control children.

Children are controllable because they are weak and dependent, a condition underscored by the practice of keeping them unproductive and out of the economic mainstream of society. When we are able to back off from the need to control them, they stand to gain not only financial rewards, but the dignity which derives from work and achievement. With it will come a new measure of respect from adults, and more importantly, a new measure of respect for themselves.

Describing this effect on Mexican versus Mexican-American children, Laurance Smith, a Los Angeles Probation officer, says:

> Poverty, in the monetary sense has little to do with this process. It is the sense of worthlessness and exclusion—the sociological term is alienation—that is significant.

Consider the fact, for example, that there is little delinquency among Mexican youths who live in Mexico, but plenty of it among their immigrant cousins living in our barrios. The ones who live in Mexico have a lot less spending money and often a lot less to eat, but they are proud of themselves. Why the difference?

Every 13-year-old from Sonora or Jalisco who is not in school is an apprentice in the local glass blowing shop or ironworks. He helps support his family, and his family depends on him and respects him. He has a role to play. He is a man. He is important.

The same 13-year-old, transplanted to Lincoln Heights, is not important or needed. He is a reject, an outcast. He is first informed of his status by the public schools, which do not want to understand or respect him. He is quickly branded as an unteachable, substandard person; a sure failure in life before it has ever begun.

When he looks around and sees his father unable to find work and his brother in trouble with the police, he realizes that there is no hope. He joins the legion of other angry outcasts —determined, perhaps, to at least make some noise on the way out.[1]

The suggestion that children should be free to work alongside adults in some kind of equality cannot help but evoke horrifying images of a return to the conditions of child labor in nineteenth-century sweat shops. After all, only a few decades have passed since the monumental struggle to end the exploitation of child labor was finally won, a struggle which lasted for more than a century.[2] Putting an end to child labor was such a recent achievement that millions of people now alive can recall the days in which children performed the most arduous work under the most unhealthy conditions in mines, mills, and factories. Until recently, embarrassed executives of New England textile factories would find themselves in the position of giving fifty-year service pins to employees who were not yet sixty years old.

At the turn of the century more than a third of the workers in the Southern textile mills were children, at least half of whom were between the ages of ten and thirteen. Many were under ten—some as young as four—working for as little as ten cents a day, or perhaps for as much as a dollar a day. The work day was long, beginning at sunup, often extending into the nighttime hours, with no supper and only a twenty-minute lunch break. It was not uncommon to find children wandering home after work in the early hours of the morning. During the busiest seasons, children were known to work more than eighty hours a week. Pale and sallow children could be found doing the most dangerous and noxious kinds of work, inhaling poisonous fumes and toxic dusts, working in cramped and crowded spaces, risking accidents and disease.

One of the longest and hardest-fought battles to end child labor took place in England with the attempt to prohibit the use of small boys as chimney sweeps or "climbing boys" as they were called. The dangerous practice of lowering these little boys into small, sooty chimneys began about 1550 or earlier, and the first effort to legislate in their behalf came in 1788. Unsuccessful attempts continued for the better part of a century and the exploitation of the climbing boys was not finally ended until 1875.

Ending the tragic conditions of child labor was surely a noble achievement of mankind. But history has left us with only the atrocious pictures of the abuses of children during that period and no genuine understanding of the meaning which child labor had for most people and the complicated forces which came together to bring about its abolition.

Child labor, in general, was not considered dishonorable. On the contrary, it was thought of as both economically and ethically valuable—good for the family and good for the child. Children worked as part of a family enterprise. The child accompanied his parents to their places of work, sat beside them and, often without pay, helped them achieve higher production and a larger income. Many were the children of immigrants who brought with them to this country a fierce determination to rise out of poverty and whose children were infused with that same sense of purpose.

During the days of child labor one in every six children was a full-time member of the labor force.[3] It was virtually impossible for families in deep poverty to survive unless all members worked. Child labor was seen as a way of keeping families together, made possible because parents had the right to put their children to work in the family's behalf. This parental right, deriving from the ancient right of a father to hold absolute power over the life and death of his wife and children, continues to be a force contributing to the economic exploitation of the child. To this day, money that is earned by a child belongs to his parents.

When the term "child labor" is mentioned, the picture that most often comes to mind is that of a child working in a coal mine, a textile mill, or a sweat shop in a crowded urban setting. Actually 60 percent of all child laborers worked in an agricultural setting. Considering the rampant dissatisfaction with city life today, it might be quite difficult to gather much sympathy for a child laborer who had the opportunity to be in the open air, close to the earth, harvesting crops and caring for animals on a family farm. Yet at the time of the debates over child labor, some thought it would be a genuine benefit to the child to be able to leave the arduous and lonely life of the farm for employment in the mills and factories of the city.

Child labor was brought to an end, rather, brought under government regulation, when several highly disparate forces came together. Certainly a major part was played by social activists like Florence Kelley and Jane Addams who helped make the horrors of child labor visible. They fought for its abolition with an appeal to conscience, on the grounds that children should be protected from such abuses. President Theodore Roosevelt joined with them, arguing the case as it is argued today: we must be interested in the conservation of childhood as a natural resource. Again, the child was worthy only as a potential adult.

These efforts were aided at about this time by the introduction of the psychological theories of Sigmund Freud and G. Stanley Hall. Both of these men, each in his own way, emphasized the idea that children progressed through important and predictable stages of growth. During these growth periods they were said to need special environments, attention, and stimulation in order to develop in healthy, normal ways. These ideas, along with the growing recognition by leading psychologists of the child's need to play, and the provocative educational philosophies of John Dewey which held that every child has a right to childhood, all contributed to a new and different view of children.

At this time, all the Western countries were undergoing rapid industrialization. The exploitation of children in factories and mines was more obvious—and more ugly—than their exploitation on the farms. And so was the exploitation of the adult workers. For the most part, child labor was the same as adult labor. Children worked alongside adults. Most of the abuses—the long hours, the low pay, the unsafe conditions—were also abuses against adults. For this reason it wasn't until there was a widespread concern for the exploitation of all workers (which came mainly as a result of the labor movement) that a special concern for children could be developed. There had been at the turn of the century several children's unions which met with some success in obtaining shorter hours and higher wages, but they were short-lived.

While the labor movement was instrumental in ending child labor, its role was somewhat less altruistic than that of the other reformers. Samuel Gompers, the first president of the American Federation of Labor, strongly advocated the end of child labor, but mainly to eliminate women and children from the work force so that they would no longer reduce the wages and displace the labor of men. To some extent children were forced into the labor market for the benefit of adults and forced out of it for the same reason.

Finally, the establishment of compulsory education and its remarkable success in enforcing school attendance simply prevented the kind of child labor which had been prevalent at the turn of the century.

The mill owners feared that they would not be able to survive the economic costs of losing their main source of cheap labor; the anti-Communists of that era felt that bringing in federal regulatory control of child labor would rupture family life, undermine parental authority and states' rights, and bring into being a socialism a la Marx and Engels. Despite these fears, child labor ended. It did not end with the passage in 1924 of the proposed Twentieth Amendment, which was never ratified, but shortly thereafter with various state and local legislation. Along with it ended the Dickens' character images of the unkempt child victimized by exploitive adults, forced onto the streets to work or beg or steal, the urchin who also victimized a few adults along the way. Incidentally, one of the arguments raised in favor of child labor was that honest labor in the factories was better than forcing children into surreptitious activities, into crime or into work of lesser status, such as bootblacking, selling newspapers, begging, and hawking wares on the streets.

Just as the movement to abolish child labor was caused to some extent by a new way of thinking about children, so it is again time to rethink what a child might be, might do. This time we need to enable children to exploit the system rather than to be exploited by it. We must try to think of children not simply as dependent members of the family, but as individuals who may need to achieve, to be productive, to gain necessary experience, to qualify for the next step in their plans for personal development. We must come to think of the child as a free agent.

The question of how long childhood should be

is a question in which the individual child should have some say. It is his right, and we must change our orientation from protecting children to protecting their rights.

What will all this mean? First of all, it will mean that the child will have the right to work. To work at any job, to work as an alternative to school, to work alongside adults. Today a child's economic motives cannot be acted upon, not only because compulsory education prevents full-time employment, but because the requirements for obtaining a work permit and exclusion from certain kinds of work severely limit his opportunities. Children must have access to all kinds of jobs through union membership, through training and apprenticeship, and through vocational and educational activities which permit entry into the professions.

Certainly the child should have equal pay for equal work, but for the most part they will be learning, practicing, and working at somewhat less than regular adult employment. Unless special wage arrangements can be made for apprenticeship and other kinds of training, it may be necessary to reconsider the concept of minimum wage, a concept which, contrary to most opinion, has not always benefited the poor and the oppressed groups for which it is intended. Unemployment among young blacks, for example, has climbed each time the minimum wage has been increased.

The possibility that the child could be promoted to leadership positions is more difficult to accept.

Middle-class, middle-aged white men already reject leadership from anyone unlike them: women, blacks, and the very old among others. It is disturbing even to speculate on their reactions to the prospect of children exerting leadership influence and holding positions of power and authority. Yet there are many brilliant, talented, and responsible children. Even if only one were capable of rising to a position of authority, he or she should not be denied that opportunity. It will not be easy; those positions are surrendered very slowly. Women, who have for many years made up a third of the work force, have yet to find their way into leadership positions.

While we are somewhat accustomed to children working in certain kinds of employment, their right to own and manage property is something for which we are totally unprepared. It brings with it a hornet's nest of problems requiring some very new and different ways of dealing with children. At present, a child can legally own private property, but cannot purchase real estate.

The problem is that children do not have the legal ability to make binding contracts nor to enter into solid commitments which call for responsible decision-making. Under present law, if a minor (according to some state laws minority ends at age eighteen, others at twenty-one) enters into a contract, the contract can usually be voided, merchandise can be reclaimed, and the money formerly exchanged must be returned. The parent cannot be held responsible for the business transactions of the child; the person with whom the child has conducted business is compelled to absorb the financial loss.

To engage in enterprise—not just in selling candy or newspapers, delivering telegrams or shining shoes, but to participate in all kinds of businesses from which he is now barred even as a customer, such as liquor stores or theaters—the child must be able to make binding agreements, sign mortgages, and obtain credit. Financial negotiations should be possible for children who have a proven record of responsibility.

The catch, of course, is that one can't obtain credit without having a credit record, and that one can't borrow money unless one doesn't need it. But this grim fact of life presents no double standard: it is equally frustrating to adults and children. In any case, it should be possible for children to begin to build a reputation for responsible dealings in the area of financial affairs.

For all this to work, the child must have the right to bring suit, to collect damages, and to use legal resources to settle disputes. In Michigan recent decisions recognize the rights and the ability of the child to file suit, but he or she must have an adult guardian in court. In most places a child can sue for personal injury and parents can be sued by their children for earnings even though the parent has a right to those earnings. Basically, however, a child cannot initiate court action unless an adult acts for him. This condition may change so that a child will be empowered to bring suit at any age. Furthermore, he must be able to retain an attorney, in the event that suits are brought against him.

Finally, children must act against their exploitation as consumers. They must change the ways they are treated in stores where adults are served first while they are made to stand and wait, or are shortchanged because the storekeeper takes advantage of their naivete. In the broader sense, advertisers and broadcasters must be policed to make advertising more honest—giving prices, and changing the basis of appeal to less demeaning images of children.

Again, the major barrier to the achievement of these rights for children is the difficulty we have in changing our fundamental concepts of childhood. As long as we view children as weak, innocent, and incompetent we will continue to treat them in a way that will only reinforce and confirm that view. But there are other barriers, too, particularly the existence of "protective legislation" for children.

Protective legislation is designed to make it impossible for children to suffer at the hands of adults, but, as in the case of most such legislation, the effect is exactly the opposite. While offering protection of a sort, it has successfully prevented the child from fulfilling his economic needs and has, therefore, kept him in a helpless and dependent position. The situation of children in this regard parallels the situation of women to a remarkable degree. Just as protective legislation has kept women from competing equally with men for leadership positions in business and industry, various forms of child labor legislation and compulsory education inhibit the enterprising child.

So-called protective legislation for women, which prevents employers from forcing women to lift heavy loads or work overtime and which compels these employers to provide cots in women's rest rooms and regular coffee breaks, has not only reinforced a stereotyped idea of the capabilities and limitations of women, but has also virtually guaranteed that they cannot advance to positions of greater responsibilities. As a consequence, women are paid only forty-eight percent of the pay that men receive—somtimes forty percent less than men for exactly the same work. This means that women must struggle along earning thousands of dollars less each year than their male counterparts, millions of them heading their own households on less than poverty wages. All this time they are supposedly enjoying the benefits of protective legislation which, instead of helping them, has actually harmed them, forcing them into greater dependency upon men.

The same is true of protective legislation for children. In what was generally a sincere effort to bring about the end of abusive treatment of child labor by nineteenth-century robber barons and exploitive fathers and mothers, legislators enacted many laws which now work against the child by preventing him from developing economic independence. Without financial resources he is impotent to relate to society in new ways, to make constructive changes in his environment, and to pursue self-determined life goals.

Most states have laws which prevent children under sixteen—and in some instances under eighteen—from being in public places after a 10 P.M. curfew, or from working without a special permit, parental permission, or during school hours or long hours. They cannot work on railroads or boats, or in factories, chemical plants, bars or liquor stores, variety theaters, bowling alleys, or pool halls; nor can they sell tobacco, deliver goods from a motor vehicle, or operate machinery considered to be dangerous. Boys under ten and girls under eighteen are also prevented from bootblacking, peddling, and selling newspapers; federal laws prevent them from working in interstate or foreign commerce or on government contracts. It is easy to see what the legislators were trying to do, but the effect has been to limit and subjugate rather than protect.

Ostensibly, the practices which keep children from engaging in financial activities are designed to protect them from unscrupulous businessmen and to protect businessmen from the impulsive, capricious, and irresponsible actions of children. The similarities to the women's situation are once again remarkable. Women are prohibited from financial dealings for much the same reasons. A single woman, and particularly a divorced woman, usually cannot establish bank credit, obtain major credit cards, or take out a mortgage. Like children they are dependent upon "the head of the house" even if there is none.

Admittedly we are slow, but we are at least beginning to see the evils of discriminating financially against classes of people on the basis of race or sex. To this list we must now add age, because severe discrimination takes place at both ends of the age spectrum. When it comes to financial dealings with people, each individual case must be decided on its own merits, otherwise we will be as guilty of "ageism" as we have been of racism and sexism.

Protecting society from the incompetence and recklessness of some children is not an unfounded concern. Nor is the concern for the incompetence and recklessness of some adults. Steps which do not require double standards based upon age requirements can be taken to provide that protection simply by making use of specific tests or licenses when matters of health, safety, and public welfare are involved.

Just as the child should have the right to drive an automobile if he or she can pass the stringent written and performance tests to qualify for an operator's license, tests and licensing should qualify children for other activities from which they are presently excluded. Dangerous machinery is dangerous for adults as well as children. No one should operate such machinery until proven competent.

Similarly, civil service examinations, tests for

union membership, and licensing examinations for professions can avoid excluding people on the basis of age by making the tests specific only as to the performance of the work. There are many weaknesses and evils inherent in occupational licensing but if a child can satisfy a board of professional examiners that he or she is fully competent to handle a job, then there should be no artifical age barriers preventing it.

Part of our resistance to the idea of children entering the world of business and industry is that we hate to expose them to the barbarism which characterizes at least the popular image of that world. It is likely that the cruelties, the internal warfare, and the insanities of business are no greater than in education or family life or any other human endeavor to which we readily expose children. Even if they were greater, and perhaps they are, the human climate of enterprise will only improve by making it possible for children to be there. In any case, ethical behavior shouldn't be excluded from business and industry simply because children are not present.

Obviously the implications of all this would profoundly alter our system of enterprise—perhaps even our way of life. We are forced to ask ourselves some difficult questions. What, for example, is to be the basic economic unit of our society, the family or the individual? Most of our programs are predicated on the family as the basis, but with the move for children's rights we are asked to think of the individual, particularly the child, as an independent person, separate from the time of its birth, no longer a forced member of family life, no longer dependent upon the family for financial support.

As a society, we are moving away from the utilitarian idea that financial support should be given only for one's actual or potential productivity or contribution to society and supporting the idea that individuals deserve some measure of guaranteed support simply because they are alive. This idea has been translated into economic proposals called negative income tax, guaranteed annual income, and other similar labels.[4] Such proposals always use the family income as the base. As we move toward thinking of the individual as a discrete economic unit, we will see the income go directly to the person, rather than filtering through the organizational hierarchy of the family.

There are two big problems with this. The first is, what will support the family structure, if anything? In the United States, the term "family" means nuclear family: two parents and minor children. Although, as noted previously, only one-third of Americans actually live in such arrangements, it remains our dominant image of life in the United States. We do many things to support it, such as giving income tax exemptions for dependents, but we also do many things to make it difficult to sustain, such as denying welfare payments if there is an employable male in the household. Guaranteed support given directly to individuals will permit more options and will also encourage the development of various family constellations or domestic units as ways to combine resources, including the nuclear family. As a result, no one would be trapped into family life because of economic dependence on it. Not the least of the benefits would be the end of the destructive practice of alimony and child support. The total cost is the same; the distribution is different. As we have seen in other chapters, many steps can be taken to make nuclear family life less victimizing and to permit the invention of alternative domestic units. But forcing women and children to be economically dependent on the nuclear family is both morally wrong and patently ineffective.

The other question raised by this proposal is, "What will an infant do with the money?" To take an extreme case, just to clarify the point, what if a two-month-old baby were to inherit a million dollars. Setting aside the arguments about the pluses and minuses of inheritance, the obvious incapability of the child prevents him from understanding that the money is even his. Under our present system, if the money were left in trust the trust officer of a bank would look after such monies until the child is at least twenty-one, and usually beyond that time. He protects the investment from outsiders—and from insiders for that matter. Parents cannot spend the money without going through the banker.

While it may not be ideal to have a banker acting in the child's behalf, some adults can be trusted to do so when it is clear that their mission is to do the best for the child, not just as a potential adult, but during childhood. With a lesser amount than a million dollars, say a guaranteed annual income payment, one could entrust the decision to parents, guardians, or as is the case in decisions regarding children in some Scandinavian countries, panels of children's advocates, with the stipulation that the money is to be used in the child's behalf. If we were to develop large-scale, twenty-four-hour child care programs, for example, the money could be used to support the child in this program.

In infancy there will be many decisions that must be made for the child. The social-action and legislative challenge is to create mechanisms which will be based on totally different ground rules than are now observed, mechanisms which will liberate the child to be self-determining. The incapacity of the child in infancy should only mean that extra steps must be taken to guarantee the protection of his rights.

If childhood were actually full of delight, the way it is publicized to be, a case for its prolongation could be made. Since it is not, we have little justification for extending childhood longer than any other society on earth. We now delay entry into the adult world well into the individual's twenties and thirties, if we are to include economic dependency during education as a definition of childhood. Part of the reason for this practice is to keep young people out of the labor market so that they do not compete for the limited supply of jobs which produce income. But a more positive interpretation is that adults want to make sure that children do not make decisions or engage in activities which might damage them until they are mature enough to understand the consequences and complexities of their actions. Aside from the question of whether or not adults understand those same consequences and complexities or whether indeed there is something definable as maturity, a more fundamental question is this: to what extent have we the *right* to prevent people from taking risks. Most people think society has this right and we now have laws against various forms of behavior regarded to be harmful, e.g., drug abuse. And we have laws which keep children from taking the possible risks of entering the world of work. Some day we may see that tryng to protect people in these ways actually has the opposite effect.

Perhaps in the future we will rely less on laws and more on counsel and persuasion and, in the larger sense, on better social design to help each other out of potentially self-destructive circumstances. Children are no exception in this hope. They cannot be denied the respect and dignity that can come from honest labor, cannot be forced to remain economically dependent, cannot be exluded from the world of adults and all that such contact could bring, simply because it is "not good for them."

11

The Right to Political Power

Eighty million citizens of the United States do not have the basic right of democratic citizenship, the right to participate in the political process. They are excluded because they are children. Along with all the other prohibitions in children's lives, they are prohibited by law from voting. The liberation of children requires that they be given the right to vote.

There are more children in the United States than there are adult women—our last major group to be given the vote, so that if children were to vote, the electorate would increase by a larger group than has ever been enfranchised at one time in our history. Small wonder that people regard such a prospect with trepidation.

Until recently, no person under the age of twenty-one has ever been permitted to participate as a voting member of this or any other Western society. This practice dates back a thousand years or more to the days when twenty-one years was the age of eligibility for knighthood.[1] Now, because overwhelming evidence makes it clear that the eighteen-year-old today is at least as mature and knowledgeable as the twenty-one-year-old of generations past, the voting age in the United States has been reduced to the age of eighteen. This was not accomplished without furor, debate, and considerable antagonism on both sides of the issue.

There were those who advocated that the voting age should actually be lower: sixteen, or perhaps even fourteen. But for most people, extending voting rights to age eighteen seemed a remarkable achievement, and those who favored even lower ages were glad to settle for it.

The common idea which united all parties to this debate was that there certainly should be *some* age at which a person should not be permitted to vote. Surely, they held, there must be an age at which the person is clearly immature, incompetent, and otherwise unqualified to participate in the decision-making process.

Eighteen-year-olds are now adults. The act of lowering the voting age to eighteen did not lower it into childhood but simply acknowledged that today's eighteen-year-olds are as well equipped to vote as most other adults. Voting remains an adult business, even though eighteen-year-olds can now engage in it, just as they can attend X-rated films.

Voting is not for children, the argument goes, because both adults and children must be protected from the possible dangerous effects of immature judgments. The idea of children voting is so foreign to our culture that it never occurs to us that we might be doing a great injustice by excluding them from full participation in society. We call ourselves self-governing, yet we prevent almost half of the population from voting. Because they are unable to vote, children do not have significant representation in governmental processes. They are almost totally ignored by elected representatives. Lobbyists for children's rights and politicians sympathetic to children's needs are remarkably rare. Children are no one's constituency.

To become a constituency, children must have the right to vote, not just at eighteen, but at any age. The prospect disturbs us because, in our paternalistic society, we believe that age is a reasonable basis for denying a person the right to exercise his powers of citizenship. This denial is actually inconsistent with fundamental concepts of democracy and self-government. It doesn't square with our remarkable record of achievement in moving toward a government of, by, and for the people. We take pride that previous generations were wise enough to discard property, literacy, knowledge, race, sex, and wealth as legitimate tests of one's right to vote. We do not deprive a senile person of this right, nor do we deprive any of the millions of alcoholics, neurotics, psychotics and assorted fanatics who live outside hospitals of it. We seldom ever prevent those who are hospitalized for mental illness from voting. Yet, we deprive the child.

In a free and democratic society there is no valid basis to exclude children from the decision-making process. In a discussion of censorship and self-government, philosopher Avrum Stroll makes the following case:

> There is nothing in democratic theory that requires that those that govern be rational, must be mature, must be educated, must be knowledgeable, and so forth. That these notions have been incorporated into democratic doctrine is mainly the result of a mistake—a mistake issuing from the all too easy acceptance of the paternalistic model. . . . It is not a precondition of self-government that those that govern be wise, educated, mature, responsible and so on, but instead these are the results which self-government is designed to produce. Through the process of making decisions, of making and correcting mistakes, of deliberating and reflecting upon the facts and the gamut of opinions concerning the facts, individuals learn to become responsible, learn to make wise and judicious judgments. It is these processes which lead to maturity, lead to an educated citizenry and lead to the development of responsible persons. Indeed we may say that it is only when children are given the responsi-

> bility to act in these ways that they can become mature adults and not simply grow older. As long as they remain wholly subject to parental domination they will not—in general—achieve maturity.[2]

Children need the right to vote because adults do not have their interests at heart and do not vote in their behalf. Adults neither share a child's conceptions or values, nor do they assess the problems of the world in the same way. And it should be obvious that they are certainly not meeting the physical, social, and emotional needs of children.

Even the adult who advocates on the behalf of children is, to some extent, similarly limited.[3] Child advocacy will never be adequate, never match the magnitude of the problem that it is trying to solve. Adults who have a concern for children's rights and needs can work to clarify the issues for debate, bring attention to problems, and even initiate demonstration programs involving children in self-determining activities to raise their consciousness.[4] But advocacy is not enough. It is necessary, but not sufficient; particularly when compared to the potential power of giving children the vote.

Children aren't totally devoid of power. They exercise it indirectly in the same undesirable ways that women formerly used to exercise their power: by crying, withholding affection, seducing, deceiving, etc. Certainly children can control adults in some limited way with these techniques. Everyone controls everyone else, at least to some extent. But it is more desirable to make those controls visible, explicit, and legitimate, so that living together is not a constant problem of secret maneuvering and indirect pressures. Giving children legitimate power means expanding their ability to exercise formal control, not as children, but as citizens; it's a right that should be theirs from birth.

Unfortunately, democracy and self-government are not concepts with which children have had much experience. In no institution in our society does the child have much opportunity to see self-government in action. Business and industry have not adopted any such model, though armies of social scientists and organizational consultants have tried for a generation to move these giant corporations toward democratic or participative management. Churches, by and large, continue their strong, hierarchical governments with separate but unequal facilities for children and without the participation of children in major policy decisions. Schools, both public and private, could hardly be more autocratic. Educational institutions, it is sad to say, give the child his most direct and powerful learning experiences about government. In spite of some recent improvements in the situation, student government is still a joke in most schools, even in most colleges. Within the family, even the permissive one, the adult usually dictates the activities of the child. So where does the child ever have the opportunity to understand or experience the possibilities of self-government? The answer is, Nowhere.

The problem of involving the child in decisions affecting his destiny is part of the larger problem of achieving that power for everyone. It is not solved solely by giving the child voting power in national elections, any more than voting power gives adults the full measure of self-determination that is possible. In addition to the vote, ways must be found to expand the child's power in all the basic institutions of our society. Although the changes are small, there is evidence that some institutions are opening up to greater participation of their members and relying less on authoritarian procedures as a means of dealing with people: the family has become less autocratic—even the military is resorting to arbitrary authority less than it has in the past. In general, however, the way our society's institutions are operated has little to do with self-government. The situation remains much as it has for centuries.

That these institutions reject self-government becomes apparent when one realizes how often the situation is described as *we* (the people at the top) doing something for *them* (the people at the bottom). Hearing it put that way should be a warning to us, whether the we-them is men-women, bosses-subordinates, whites-blacks, or adults-children. Such a statement could only come from the oppressor.

It would be a mistake to argue that children

should vote because they are competent to do so. Competence is not the issue, not even for adults. Children should have the right to vote because they are members of our society and because without the vote, they are deprived of the necessary attention that is given to those who have it.

Not that a case couldn't be made for the competence of children. Adults are obviously not the sole custodians of truth and reason and are inclined, as children are not, to accept the status quo. The clear-eyed perception of children can often expose superficialities and get through to basics. The movement for students' rights which began in the colleges and has now moved down to high schools and even elementary schools has demonstrated that remarkably mature judgments can come from these responsible, knowledgeable, forward-looking students. A good many writers in the 1960's (a bit overenthusiastically perhaps) believed that young people were in a better position to make the necessary changes in our society than were adults. But these arguments are essentially beside the point. Suggesting that children are equal to adults in their ability to cast intelligent votes is absurd and invites unnecessary debate. Children should vote (as should others who are now deprived of the vote, such as convicts, ex-offenders, and resident aliens) simply because they are functioning members of society whose needs are ignored.

The argument that children should not vote because they lack the ability to make informed and intelligent decisions is valid only if that standard is applied to all citizens. If the vote is limited to those who can demonstrate that they possess sufficient knowledge and intelligence to responsibly decide both their own and everyone else's future, we might not have what democratic theorists would call self-government, but we would have what is, in theory at least, a fair system. The unfairness shows up when we confront the question of who should construct the test, and when we discover that no matter how complete the test, it systematically excludes certain classes of people who do not have a facility with the language, do not have equal access to schools and to information. Such systems seem so rational, yet they inevitably become elitist rather than democratic.

The typical viewpoint is that voting is a privilege and should be granted only to those fully trapped members of our society who are employed, married, and paying a mortgage. From the beginning of our experiment in democracy Alexander Hamilton and others of the founding fathers suggested that the vote be limited to those who had something to lose.[5] Gradually we have come to see that it must not only go to people who have something to lose, but also, and perhaps especially, to those who have something to gain.

The existing situation in which the people who are in power are able to exercise the vote and the people who are out of power, for one reason or another, are unable to do so, needs to be rectified.

To make society work well, we must meet the needs of the marginal people. And the largest group of ignored, invisible, marginal people are children.

Because there are so many millions of children who would vote if the opportunity were theirs, a great many fears arise in the minds of adults. It is impossible to allay everyone's fears about risk or change because the vote is not given on the basis of maintaining the status quo. The vote is granted because there is no ideological alternative. Once we recognize the injustice and illegitimacy of denying the vote to an oppressed group, we amend our constitution to enfranchise them, as we have several times in our history, e.g., with blacks and women.

The major fear is that the children's vote will be reckless, selfish, and irresponsible. It is, however, difficult to believe that children would vote more irresponsibly than adults have voted. Even if children voted for a big rock candy mountain, it would hardly outdo adults for ridiculous expenditures. Actually, the problem is just the opposite of what we fear. The likelihood is that children will not vote as a bloc at all. They will vote as their parents do. Women, for example, have had the vote for more than fifty years and have yet to vote independently, in their own behalf. They are inclined to vote with their husbands and fathers. For over a hundred years, to the extent that they have been permitted to vote at all, blacks have voted with Southern whites. Newly enfranchised groups probably don't vote selfishly enough. They tend not to vote as a bloc and thereby leave their cause underrepresented and their needs unmet. If the family did dominate the child's vote, it would simply expand the power of adults in a systematic way and would probably not produce any major changes in already established voting patterns.

Another question is, Should the child have the right to hold high office, the right to vote for himself? Again the answer is yes. A person cannot be denied the right to seek and hold office simply because of age. It may be legitimate to require special qualifications of a citizen who desires a particular role in that society, as long as the tests are applied equally, without discrimination against classes of people, and as long as the qualifications have been established by the consent of the governed. If these conditions of the democratic process were met, then tests such as the ability to obtain signatures endorsing one's candidacy, to pass an examination similar to civil service examinations for nonelective offices in government might be legally applied.

The physical, biological, and mental limitations of infancy and early childhood will always restrict very young children to some extent. Their obvious inability to vote is no exception. But every effort must be made to change the voting procedures so that they are easier for children, no matter how incompetent or incapable we judge them to be.

The prospect of enfranchising children helps us to see more clearly the fundamental problems with voting as a way of achieving consent. Studies of the voting behavior of adults show that only a small portion of potential voters actually do vote and very few understand the issues upon which they are voting. Armed with these facts, some critics argue that we are foolish to try to govern ourselves with the democratic process. Yet we have managed to stumble along somehow, even with this very imperfect voting system. Things sort themselves out eventually; the errors we make are not fatal; the checks and balances in the system seem to work fairly well. There are, however, many actions we could take to make the voting system work better so that adults as well as children could vote more intelligently. We could, for example, simplify the language and wording of the ballots. It is estimated that on some ballot propositions less than 10 percent of the voters have even the vaguest understanding of the issues. We could also reduce the number of decisions put before the voter. Almost all of the decisions made in the government are not made in the voting booth anyway, and the electorate can maintain a considerable amount of control even though not every issue is voted upon. Changes could be made in the manner of presentation, in the design and display of choices before the voter. Most importantly, issues could be clustered within a general point of view, and at the same time clearly different options could be described so that the voter would do more than approve or disapprove, but could select from among expanded alternatives the kind of future he wants for himself and for society.

Different methods using new communications technology could be employed to facilitate voting at both local and national levels. Eventually local problems could be solved using two-way cable television, enabling everyone in a neighborhood or small community to have both audio and video contact with each other as they express themselves on issues of local importance. The same system would permit electronic input from the individual viewers, in this instance, voters, directly into the broadcasting studio.

On the national level it is increasingly possible, by means of combined computer-video technology, to have plebiscite voting whereby people express themselves immediately and frequently on various issues, via their television sets, telephones, or home computer terminals. But we don't have to wait for this kind of installation in the home in order to make vast improvements in the voting system. Technology already exists in practically every home in America for completely different kinds of educational experiences which could be fundamental to new voting procedures. What would otherwise be very expensive terminal equipment, if one had to install it now, can be found today in the homes of every socioeconomic, racial, religious, and age group in America, because in almost every home there is a television set, a telephone, and a newspaper. These communications instruments have seldom been used in combination, and never for problem-solving or decision-making. Using the technique of simulation, it would be possible to involve people in playing games about the future, presenting the major problems of the nation as television dramas. Viewers could play roles in these dramas, assigned by their local newspapers, which would also provide instructions in the playing of each role. They would then act out their roles in response to the televised situation by telephoning their ideas and decisions into a centralized computer which compiles and relays them to the broadcasting studio, making it possible for the viewer actually to determine the outcome of the simulated drama while it is being presented.

There are numerous ways in which technology can be applied to the problem of eliciting the intelligence of the American electorate, both adult and child. New and exciting ways. Some involve high technology, some low technology, but all require major expenditures of money. We haven't even begun to experiment with the new possibilities of radically altering the voting system, but they all show promise of making participation in the decision-making process broader, more effective and more rewarding than it has ever been.

Unless new ways are found to increase the total quality of participation in voting at the same time that the electorate is broadened to include children, we will find ourselves with decreasing influence in our government. The inevitable price we pay for broad-based participation in government, and we are paying it now, is relinquishment of most decisions to a small group of leaders. It works paradoxically. If voting were limited to those who are well-informed on the issues, then more decisions could be put before these voters. If, however, we want to extend the vote to all members of society without asking for tests of literacy, knowledge, and emotional maturity, then we must restrict the number and complexity of the decisions these voters are asked to make, which results in our giving a great deal of executive power to a few people. To avoid this we need to employ better methods of gaining the intelligent participation of the total electorate.

No system will work without individual responsibility, but individual responsibility will not work without systemic change, without redesigning the system within which we express our collective wishes. It is not enough to ask people to vote, to study the issues, etc. In addition, we must make intelligent participation both possible and desirable. Progress is learning to go both directions at once.

Bringing children into the electorate will be a difficult experience for everyone. Not all the fears are unjustified. We are understandably reluctant to risk overburdening our experiment in self-government. But there is no alternative. We now have a new awareness, a new consciousness of children. The very experiment we want to protect requires that we act on this new consciousness. The system has worked well enough to have enabled us to see children in these new ways. Now that they are visible, that same democratic system must expand to include them. That is what democracy is all about.

12

The Right to Justice

Every year a million children get into trouble with the law. One out of every nine children will go through the juvenile court system before age eighteen. One out of every six boys. At any given time, about one hundred thousand children are in some kind of jail. Some are held illegally; many have not committed any kind of crime; most have not done anything that would be considered a crime if done by an adult; and none have been given a fair trial with due process of law.

Whatever is wrong with our overall system of justice, law enforcement, the courts, and penology is doubly true when applied to children. Most people believe that the juvenile justice system is more benign, when in fact it is more unfair, more cruel, more arbitrary, and more repressive.

How do children find their way into this kind of trouble in the first place? Some admittedly have robbed, assaulted, raped, and murdered. But the vast majority are apprehended, sentenced, and imprisoned for having done something which would not be thought of as a crime if committed by an adult. Most children get in trouble for truancy, running away, curfew violations, sexual promiscuity, incorrigibility. They are held in detention, without bail, often illegally, under the loose terms, INS (In Need of Supervision) or FOC (Awaiting Further Order of the Court). Eighty percent of the girls committed to the youth authority in California are termed "incorrigible," thought to be beyond the control of their parents or school authorities.

In some states by simply filling out a form, any parent can have his child locked up in the local juvenile detention house. "Beyond the control" of adult authority is so loosely defined that many children are taken into custody by juvenile officers merely because their parents are sick and tired of them, or because the child has disobeyed a parental order, such as "Stop going out with Jimmy." Howard James, in his book *Children in Trouble,* from which these examples were taken, discusses the definition and language of juvenile proceedings, citing the case of a nine-year-old boy who was found exploring sexually with an eight-year-old girl and was booked for "assault with intent to ravish." One nine-year-old twisted another's arm, took twenty-five cents and was booked for "highway robbery."

The police assigned to the juvenile detail (the Mickey Mouse detail) too often decide who goes to court. If the parents had called another agency first, say a social welfare agency, the child probably would not have to go to court or to reform school. Once the police machinery begins cranking, however, it is all too likely that the child will be arrested, acquire a police record, and quite possibly go to some kind of prison.

From the discussion so far one might develop the idea that all that is necessary to do is to separate the "real" delinquent children from those whose crimes are trivial. That in itself is not easy to do. A child's actions do not seem trivial to the parent who has finally, in desperation, called the police. And who is to judge, who makes the decisions? We have already seen that it is too often decided by the police officer.

There is an even more difficult problem, having to do with how we think about delinquency, what we define as delinquent, and what it means in this society. We may have to come to some very different ways of viewing delinquent behavior, even to the point of valuing children's behavior that we have previously regarded as troublemaking and wrong.

In recent years, we in this society have had the experience of changing our attitudes, and to some extent our behavior, toward large groups of oppressed people—notably women and blacks—who made us realize that our stereotyped ways of thinking about them had become their ways of thinking about themselves. But in the rebellious process of raising their own consciousness, they raised ours. We now think differently about them, value them in new ways, just as they value themselves. Today we value the challenging and demanding black who will no longer shuffle and look away from the white man. We are coming to value the assertive woman who will not resort to manipulation by being coquettish. We respect their new concepts of themselves, their unwillingness to continue to perform the way society expects them to, and their determination to take control of their lives. Soon we may come to value the child who also has that strength of purpose.

In the future we may view differently the incorrigible child, the stubborn child, the "acting out" child, the runaway child. Depending upon its nature and target we may even think differently about violence and vandalism. We shall certainly have to reassess our prejudiced attitudes about juvenile gangs. Shulamith Firestone claims that "Gangs are the only modern children's groups that are self-directed: the term *gang* has an ominous sound for good political reasons."[1] We may no longer categorize a rebellious, runaway child who is a member of a gang as necessarily troubled. In the world of children's liberation, the good, well-adjusted child may be less far along in his own consciousness-raising, in his own development toward maturity.

The court which is now charged with the responsibility of deciding the fate of children in trouble is a special invention designed to protect them from the harsh practice of adult criminal justice. Juvenile courts were established in most states shortly after the turn of the century; the first one started in Illinois in 1899.[2] They were meant to provide the child with a fatherly judge, who, with his arm around the youngster, would work out a solution to his problems. Unfortunately, the system did not work out that way. From the moment he is picked up by the police to the moment he is discharged by the correctional officer, the child is treated as a criminal. The "fatherly judge" is too often an inadequate, ill-prepared, overworked person who must daily make dozens of life-altering decisions (literally one every five minutes or so) without the benefit of anything approaching careful investigation. He is therefore forced to follow the recommendations of the juvenile officer or the probation officer.

Before the United States Supreme Court's famous Gault decision in 1967, the child had no right to any of the protections adults have as they face courtroom proceedings. Justice Abe Fortas wrote the majority opinion in the Gault case in which eight out of nine of the judges agreed that at least some of the constitutional rights of adults were to apply to children; that in any juvenile case the child has the right not to testify in a self-incriminating way, the right to have the benefit of an attorney, a court-appointed attorney if the child's family cannot afford one, and the right to cross-examine any witness who testifies against him.

This landmark decision was made as the result of a case brought before the Supreme Court in which a fifteen-year-old boy, Gerald Gault, was given an indeterminate sentence, served two years, and could have served six years in a prison or reformatory, for making obscene phone calls, a crime which carries a maximum of two months in jail for any adult. The gross injustice of this general procedure was finally recognized so that today, although juveniles do not have all the rights of due process, such as a jury trial, adversary proceedings, and the right to bail, the child does have some new protections.

In practice, however, the Gault decision has not been implemented to any great extent, and any investigation made by the appointed defense attorney is cursory. Ordinarily, if there is an attorney protecting the children in court at all, he is assigned to the court, not to the particular child, and his job is to represent all, or at least many, of the children on that court's docket.[3] This means that he can neither prepare the child's case, nor follow it through, for either he or the child may be assigned a different courtroom on the day set for another hearing.

Once again the attempt to do what is "good for the child," to protect his welfare rather than his rights, is not ultimately to the child's benefit. In dealing with children's rights what is good for the child is, to some extent, beside the point. Focusing on the welfare of the child rather than on his full rights to citizenship leads us to create all kinds of protective legislation and privilege which in the long run actually militates against the child. Whenever we deny people their civil rights in an effort to "protect" them, we usually wind up having made their plight even worse. We have seen this process come to light with respect to the achievement of women's rights. Opposition to the Equal Rights Amendment has been couched in statements such as "but this will endanger women, they will be subject to the draft, to lifting heavy packages, they won't get social security early." In trying to be protective of women, legislators were perpetuating a system of discrimination whose effects were far worse than the imagined problems of equal rights. So we might learn a lesson from women's liberation and be particularly careful about our inclination to do something *special* for children. This paternalistic attitude tends to get us into more trouble than it gets us out of, and we are in great trouble with our present system of juvenile justice.

As unfair as the juvenile laws and juvenile courts may be, the real horrors of the system are in its prisons. They are never called prisons, of course, but have euphemistic names such as juvenile detention homes or industrial training schools. But they are prisons in every sense of the word: with guards, barbed wire, locked rooms, and solitary confinement. On any given day there are hundreds of children held in solitary confinement; some are there for weeks. Children who are sent to these institutions, whether or not they have committed a "crime," are forced to go through the same humiliating procedures as all other criminal offenders: they must give up their personal belongings, strip for physical examinations, take a shower, put on a prison uniform, and so on.

The conditions in these institutions are often deplorable, even for prisons; there are wretched living arrangements, sickening floggings, and other cruel and degrading treatment. But the real shame of the system is that most of the children who are there haven't committed a crime in any adult sense of the term. Many have committed no crime at all, but are there because they can no longer live at home with their parents, and there is no other place to send such a child. Judges don't want to make such assignments, but they literally have no alternatives. Howard James describes a typical situation:

> Take the case of 13-year-old Pauline, who appeared in Judge J. McNary Spigner's court, Columbia, S.C., in 1969. A check by court workers disclosed that not only was her mother a drunk, but she was also a tramp who took up with every man who came along. Often the neighbors saw her chasing the child, half-running, half-staggering, screaming and swearing and beating her with a broom. The

> youngster was growing up without proper food or clothing, living more like a wild animal than a human being. Then Pauline began hanging around with Susan, a 20-year-old unwed mother. Both were picked up when a neighbor complained that Pauline and the older girl smashed her windows and harassed her in other ways. This brought Pauline to court, and eventually she was sent to reform school. In committing her, Judge Spigner said, in his order:
>
> "This Court has no place for this child. It cannot find a foster home that will accept her. It has no home of its own where this girl can stay. So she is committed to the School for Girls (a reform school), which in this instance is being used as an orphanage. Substantially the child is being punished for the misdeeds of her mother. The Court knows this is wrong, but it has no alternative!"[4]

It should be evident from the nature of the crimes they have committed that children who have been sent to institutions for truancy, incorrigibility and the like are victims of a troubled family life. Going to prison at all is bad enough, but having a family which rejects them makes the prison situation doubly difficult. Because all juveniles' sentences are indeterminate, that is, they have no fixed time of servitude, these children actually spend *more* time in prison than their age mates who have committed more antisocial crimes such as assault, theft, or rape, but who can get out early because their families will welcome them back.

It is well known that these institutions do not rehabilitate children. In the entire California Youth Authority and county camps there is not one psychiatrist performing treatment duty.[5] These prisons are more likely to train children for a life of crime. Children sent to these institutions begin to think of themselves as bad, and as they put in more time, with higher and higher delinquent status, they come to identify themselves as criminals. Indeed, fully 70 percent of all those children who enter the youth authority repeat their offenses and graduate to adult penal institutions.

The entire juvenile justice system is not working, and it will not work. No matter how much we invest in our present programs. No matter how much we accelerate our current approaches to these problems. It will not work because it is part of a larger system of criminal justice which is not working. Law enforcement, criminal courts, and the penal system in the United States are a multibillion dollar failure. To apply more or less the same impoverished strategies to juveniles that we do to adults is equally scandalous. Children and adults should receive equal treatment, but we can no longer continue to treat either as we do.

We Americans continue to live with absurd and dangerous strategies for reducing crime because we cannot face two basic facts: (1) crime is largely the product of our negligence of the problems of poverty, of the inner city, and of minority groups, and (2) our police, our courts, and our prisons all serve to escalate rather than reduce crimes of violence.

The way our system works is largely invisible to the average American who reads the newspapers and watches television. To him the police seem to be good at catching criminals, the courts seem to be bending over backwards to be fair, and the prisons seem to have our most dangerous criminals under lock and key are are doing a heroic, if not always successful, job of rehabilitating the rest. All of this is a total distortion of reality, full of wishful thinking, myth, and a good measure of propaganda.

The facts are that most crimes are not even known to the police, let alone solved by them. The courts try only a small fraction of those people arrested, the rest have been persuaded to plead guilty, often to a lesser offense, so as not to further overload the system; the courts discriminate grossly against members of minority groups who are brought before them for trial and sentencing. Prisons incarcerate only a small percentage of those who commit even the serious crimes, rehabilitate almost none, but instead serve as training ground for more serious crime. Most criminals are at large.

As preposterous as it seems, there is some reason to believe that we might actually experience less crime if we were to do away with all law enforcement agencies, all criminal courts and all prison systems.

We are not likely to do that, nor is it the correct action to take. But because each of these systems works so badly and in fact each creates so much crime, we should, if only as an exercise in planning a better system, evaluate the risks involved in scrapping the entire machinery.

Consider these facts: most crimes are not even reported—for various reasons. Members of minority groups often feel that the police are against them. Others fear the visibility and involvement. Many people feel it is useless to report crimes, or they simply take crime for granted, as part of their environment. Only one in every ten rapes is ever reported because of the humiliation suffered by the woman who makes such a report. Of the serious crimes reported, ranging from murder to auto theft, only one in nine leads to a conviction. Even in the cases of murder, which, more than other crimes, tends to be reported to the police, the conviction rate is only one in four.[6] Considering the fact that burglary is difficult to prove and only about one in five is ever reported, the chances against conviction are about one hundred and fifty to one. Because so many serious crimes are unreported, probably only about one in fifty leads to a conviction. Of those convicted only one in four will be sent to prison. The length of stay in prison for those so sentenced is not likely to be more than a few years. Life sentences average seven years and terms for other serious crimes average less than three years.

Although we cannot know how many unreported or unsolved crimes a convicted person may have committed (some surely have committed dozens, perhaps hundreds), only a very small percentage, perhaps one or two percent, of the people who commit serious crimes are in prison. The rest are at large. Prison wardens and guards estimate that even among those imprisoned only 10 or 15 percent present any real danger to society. This is partly because the easiest people to apprehend and convict are those unprofessional criminals who have committed crimes of passion. The professional member of organized crime is seldom caught.

To get a more graphic picture of the risks we run in dismantling the system, suppose there are a hundred criminals at large in your community. If all the prisons were emptied, that figure might increase to one hundred and two, and these additional two are not necessarily the most dangerous.

The fundamental question is whether or not, with all its faults, the system may still deter people from criminal behavior. No doubt there are features of the system that do deter. People driving in their cars tend to slow down when they see a police car ahead of them. Whether more serious crimes are deterred, or whether most people refrain from serious crime because of the knowledge that they might go to prison, is a question that can never be answered. We do know that the penal system is a school for crime for both adults and children. Criminal behavior escalates from the type of learning which takes place inside these prisons. It is an expensive and dehumanized system which works most tragically against children, blacks, and other minority groups.

As everyone knows by now, it is next to impossible for a rich white man to go to jail. He has enough power to be able to avoid it, and because he is similar to the judge in important ways he needs to do less to avoid it. Convicts who are incarcerated for trying to overthrow the government by force are not the only political prisoners. Anyone whose sentence tends to be longer because of society's racist and sexist views is, in a sense, a political prisoner. He or she lacks the power of the rich white man. The system is to that extent a political system, responding by discriminatory action to the power differences in society. Crime itself is at least partly a political act, both to the criminal who is trying to redistribute power or wealth, and to the society which defines crime as that which threatens the power of our corporate, educational, financial, government, and community institutions. This is true whether we are talking about "big crime," influence peddling, tax fraud, government contract irregularities, or more common street crime associated with the inner city. Going into a bank with a note demanding that the teller fill a paper bag with money is a crime, but to take the same money through regular borrowing procedures, paying the bank 18 percent interest, is not.

Social researcher Albert Biderman argues that

in spite of what we constantly hear and what one would ordinarily believe, increasing crime rates are associated with social progress, affluence and inflation, for example. Increased affluence means that there are more things to be desired and stolen, while increased inflation means that these things are worth more. What was once considered a petty crime, such as stealing a bicycle, is now a serious crime because the bicycle has increased in value enough to move it out of one category into another.

There are other examples: automobiles have made us mobile, transient, urban, and anonymous, all of which increase the crime rates. Better policing methods increase the crime rates because more crimes are discovered and reported. The development of insurance programs which encourage people to report crimes that would not otherwise have been reported increases the crime rate.

In an advanced society there is more homogeneity, more people adhere to social norms and less deviation is permitted. Much of what might have passed unnoticed in earlier days or in rural settings is no longer acceptable and has actually become criminal behavior. The crime rate goes up. Even the growth of civil rights for minorities has contributed in part to the increased crime rate. For example, programs which reduce the mortality rate of blacks increase the percentage of people who live in the areas with the highest crime rate and who commit more crimes, as both juveniles and adults. The most unbelievable fact is that even with the increase in crime statistics which, as we have seen, comes with progress, people are becoming more law-abiding. Biderman has shown that the crime statistics offered by those who benefit by high crime rates such as police departments and the FBI are highly suspect; they are often not even corrected for population growth, let alone for all the other variables that alter the interpretation.[7] Just as we are led to believe that there is less highway safety because of the increased number of accidents reported, when in fact highway safety is greater than ever, we are also led to believe that more people are breaking the law when, in reality, people are more law-abiding, particularly among the groups with the highest crime rate. Learning to suspect all statistics is a healthy beginning.

Most Americans have never in their entire lifetimes witnessed, in person, any violent crime such as a shooting or stabbing, yet we have what is often called a culture of violence. Indeed, by some standards, it is violent. Compared to many other nations, certainly.

Americans grow up in an atmosphere of violence: corporal punishment in the home, where the parent slaps the child for hitting another child, exclaiming at the same time, "Don't hit!" Corporal punishment in the school, where there is a tradition of using violence to force obedience to authority. Violence on television—the average child sees thirteen thousand televised murders between the ages of five and thirteen; television presents an act of destruction every twenty seconds, 79 percent of which are rewarded. Films, television, and comic books, just about everything that the child sees or hears or reads almost always shows violence as the ultimate and best solution to human conflict. We are fascinated with violence; we applaud it, find it exhilarating. We are excited by gangs, by the Mafia, by organized crime; Frank Sinatra is all the more glamorous for his rumored underworld connections, Norman Mailer for stabbing his wife. Violence and macho, we respect those who can handle both. And we are prepared for violence with perhaps as many as two hundred million guns in the private possession of Americans.

It is not surprising, then, that we bring a cops and robbers mentality into our thinking about crime control. We believe that above all else we must catch criminals. If violence is necessary, don't hesitate to use it. So our police are heavily armed and are frequently guilty of shooting to death suspects running from the scene of a crime who refuse to stop when ordered. Some of them are youngsters. Police have been known to shoot deaf people under even less suspicious conditions. Shopkeepers want to get into the act, so they keep hidden guns in the event of a robbery attempt. Many are killed trying to use them to prevent a $50 loss. Others, more successful, are honored by having their picture in the paper for killing the would-be robber. We think nothing of a robbery attempt escalating into a killing, as long as it is the robber who is killed. All this to curb crime and violence.

It is against the backdrop of this insane attempt to cope with the total crime problem in the United States that we must understand the special problems of juvenile justice. It turns out that juvenile problems aren't so special, but only exaggerated forms of adult problems.

There are actions to take which might benefit both adults and children—but because they either ask us to look at situations which we would prefer not to see, or to move in directions exactly the opposite from our present course, they may not be actions we are willing to take.

First, we must recognize the major source of trouble. Ultimately no solution to these problems exists short of solving the overriding problems of poverty, race, density, and health—the dominating problems of the inner city which create crime. Former United States Attorney General Ramsey Clark puts it this way:

> Most crime in America is born in environments saturated in poverty and its consequences: illness, ignorance, idleness, ugly surroundings, hopelessness. Crime incubates in places where thousands have no jobs, and those who do have the poorest jobs; where houses are old, dirty and dangerous; where people have no rights. A fraction of our people live there—less than

> one in five—but they number 40 million, more than our total population of a century ago. More people are jammed in several city blocks today than populated our biggest city in 1787. Probably four in five of all serious crimes flow from places of extreme poverty and most are inflicted on the people who live there. Yet most who live in poverty never commit a serious crime.[8]

Second, we can rethink our way of life, our discriminating practices against all marginal people, our love of violence, our preoccupation with growth and affluence, our acquisitiveness in owning automobiles, private property, and countless objects which we hope will improve our lives.

Third, we can decriminalize all so-called "victimless" or consensual crimes, such as prostitution, gambling and narcotics—take them off the books completely. The same should be done for the juvenile crimes of incorrigibility, truancy, running away, curfew violation, all of which rob children of their rights to self-determination. This means that a variety of alternative living arrangements will have to be provided for children who cannot or will not live with their parents.

Fourth, we can involve the people who are part of the problem in its solution. Ex-offenders can be utilized more for the rehabilitation of other offenders. This can apply in areas of juvenile justice. Children can be of great help to other children as demonstrated in schools where children teach each other and in clinics such as the Southern California Counseling Center where children administer their own treatment program for themselves and other children.

Fifth, instead of moving in the direction of creating a locked-door and armed society, we can perform the difficult task of making ourselves more vulnerable. This may seem to be doing just the opposite of what we feel like doing, but it is a more promising strategy than escalation. We can disarm the police and ourselves, refrain from asking police to do the extremely dangerous job of apprehending all criminals and of enforcing the unenforceable. Instead we can upgrade the police to professionals who will deal with the more complicated problems of helping people live together in order and peace. Perhaps we can even test the limits of our ability to live without prisons. We will have to experiment with this gradually because the possible consequences are unpredictable. It is surely difficult to believe that we will not need to forcefully incarcerate *some* people. But the State of Massachusetts has abandoned altogether the practice of imprisoning juveniles and the recidivism rate has consequently dropped sharply. Perhaps it is not too much to hope that we will someday be able to deal with all of our problems of criminal justice, both adult and child, with equally bold and humane programs.

While it is possible and necessary to analyze, interpret, and suggest, the complex problem of some people not doing what most others want them to do or think they should do will not be eliminated with the application of some theory or technology. Osburn Segerberg, Jr. concludes a report on juvenile muggers with:

> . . . so while the fact of increasing juvenile violence stands out clearly and alarmingly, even the best interpretations seem familiar and not very helpful. One definition of innocence is the belief that for every problem there is a solution. In this case, we may have passed beyond the age of innocence and entered into a troubled transition, into maturity.[9]

The problem does not end with a concern for juvenile justice in criminal matters. It only begins there. Arbitrary legal practices extend into every phase of children's lives. Matters such as custody and medical care rarely involve any serious attention to the needs and preferences of the child. The extension of civil liberties to protect the child from invasion of privacy and to guarantee his freedom of speech, of expression, of the press are equally infrequent. Schools are among the worst offenders. Although the Supreme Court has held to the contrary, in actual practice the child loses his constitutional rights when he enters the school grounds. He is in a situation of double jeopardy; he can be punished both by the school and by the state.

In spite of the growing amount of civil rights

legislation and precedent-setting decisions which favor children, as well as the publication of a number of books and pamphlets outlining their rights, most children are simply not aware of the situation. Being children they do not expect fairness or justice, nor do their parents. As Edgar Friedenberg says in his book *The Dignity of Youth and Other Atavisms,* "It is idle to talk of civil liberties to adults who were systematically taught in adolescence that they had none; and it is sheer hypocrisy to call such people freedom loving."[10] Children do have some rights, but they must fight to keep those and to obtain the rest. To do this they have to feel that they deserve those rights. Most do not feel that now. Until the child comes to own the Constitution as his, as applying to him as much as any citizen, until he feels he has the right to full participation in our society and the guarantees and protections that come with that participation, until he believes that he can demand fair treatment in every institution, the battle for children's rights will not have reached its primary objective.

13

Redesigning the American Way of Life

Whatever else may be wrong with a child, his fundamental disability is that he is a child. In comparison to the overwhelming problems of being a child, almost everything else is less important. His behavior, his relations with others, his chance for happiness, all are determined for the most part by the socially-imposed limits of being a child. So whether we are interested in curing a child's "pathological" problem of hyperactivity or delinquency, or in achieving a child's higher potential for creativity or genius, the major barrier to overcome is the oppressive condition of childhood itself.[1]

We conspire as a society to keep children weak, innocent, helpless, and dependent. We indoctrinate, patronize, ignore, dominate, prohibit, compel, incarcerate, and abuse them. We deny them the opportunity for self-determination, economic independence, political power, sexual experience, self-education, and equal justice. We discriminate against them in every conceivable way and then have the gall to exhibit concern over their developing a healthy identity, a positive self-concept.

Until society's views as to what a child might be undergo radical change, the child is trapped, a prisoner of childhood. Under these conditions, a child is not able to take much responsibility for his behavior, nor can his parents or teachers. All are able only to play out carefully prescribed roles in a scenario written by society. A child cannot liberate himself; a parent cannot liberate his child; a school cannot liberate its students. This is not a problem that can be worked out in isolation. It is a pervasive social problem that must be dealt with by society as a whole. Individual action will be necessary, but it can never be sufficient. Only concerted action taken on many fronts can enable children to escape their prisons. We either do this all together or it won't be done.

Even taking what seems to be a small step in the right direction can prove ultimately to be the wrong tactic. Understandably we all want to "do something" about a problem that has come to be important to us. That is the traditional American Way. When we discover a problem, our immediate concern is "What can I do about it right now?"

This peculiarly American approach to life is deep within us all. It reflects our problem-solving mentality, our conviction that if there is something wrong we can and should fix it, the sooner the better. This quality is what distinguishes us as Americans, or possibly as Westerners, and is not an inconsiderable factor in our progress as a nation.

When it comes to social problems and human affairs, however, we will take action quickly, but only in a token way. We believe that it is "better to light one candle than to curse the darkness." Once we are alerted to a problem we try to think of ways that we can help even if it is only to do something within our own limited resources.

In the long run, however, that may not be the most helpful approach. We are prone to rush in with partial solutions, believing that we are indeed helping but actually making the problem worse. Our small steps have actually postponed the more system-wide solutions that might be possible if we only took the time to think about the problem. Our response to the environmental crisis is a case in point. People who grasped only a vague notion of the problem were quick to want to do something about it. So they recycle their aluminum cans, which actually has no effect on the problem at all. That in itself is not bad. But because people believe that it helps, if only in a small way, because they think that the solution lies in an accumulation of efforts at that level, the ultimate confrontation of the fundamental and complex ecological problems, and the major changes in our way of life that will be required are postponed, perhaps dangerously so.

We are not good at stewing about our problems. We hurry to find quick solutions before we really understand the full dimensions of the situation. We want to light our one candle when we should be cursing the darkness—at least until we experience that darkness and develop an appreciation for the magnitude of the problem we are trying to solve. Only in that way will we ultimately be contributing to the solution rather than to the problem.

A new kind of revolution in our society is needed today. Not just a children's movement, but a revolution that embraces all oppressed groups. Not some vague, general movement for "human liberation," but a revolution that can deal comprehensively with the broad problems of society and at the same time respond to the unique problems of each particular movement for liberation. Today, for the most part, each movement represents itself and no other. Most people who are interested in social change, then, are members of what might be called single-issue constituencies. Blacks are for Black Liberation, gays are for Gay Liberation, women for Women's Liberation, etc. Each feels that the existence of the other, however worthy, somehow dilutes his own efforts and consequently there is little collaboration or coalition.

Unless we develop a more comprehensive approach to these problems we will continue to be in a position of trying for solutions one at a time, one liberation movement after another. That approach will only give us what we already have, revolutions of consciousness without revolutions of action. We in America are good at that, raising our consciousness but not changing our behavior. We are now aware of poverty and racial problems in the United States, yet in spite of our changed rhetoric about the issues, we have not acted on the problems. As a result the position of the black relative to the white in our society has actually worsened in the past twenty years, and there is a greater discrepancy between righ and poor now than before poverty programs were instituted. Our token efforts to make changes in a steadily deteriorating situation did not move us fast enough to stay even, let alone improve. In order for children's liberation or any liberation movement to succeed we must develop ourselves into a multiple-issue constituency enabling all of us to work together to build a society capable of responding to the needs of the many rather than the few.

When all of the people who consider themselves—for one reason or another—to be marginal members of society are added together, it includes just about everybody. We will not make a mistake in trying to redesign society to fit marginal people like children because such a design will work for everybody. But designing society with an eye only on that mythical person in the center doesn't work for anybody.

Imagine a piece of paper across the top of which are listed all the people represented by liberation movements: blacks, Chicanos, Indians, Asians, women, men, children, old people, gay people, those incarcerated against their will in mental hospitals, prisons, nursing homes, schools, the physically handicapped, etc. Down the side of the paper would be listed the basic dimensions of our way of life, our institutions: communication, education, government, housing, transportation, public health, business, recreation, law enforcement, etc. If you were to draw lines across and down the page separating each of these headings, you would have formed a grid or matrix full of little rectangles. Each of these little cells in the matrix would represent the intersection of a particular liberation movement with one of the basic institutions, e.g., women and housing, blacks and public health, children and law enforcement. While we don't ordinarily think of these movements and institutions in this way, it turns out that there are important implications for every cell in the matrix. To take examples: at the intersection of women and housing, we can see the woman's problem of being ghettoized in the suburbs, in a nuclear family house with no community facilities such as child care centers, communal kitchens, etc. At the intersection of blacks and public health, we can see the need for attention to higher infant mortality, special diseases such as sickle cell anemia, inner city sanitation problems. With respect to children and law enforcement we can find need for the reexamination of juvenile justice procedures, children's prisons, police harassment. Even an intersection with seemingly unlikely implications, such as Gay Liberation and transportation, there are valid concerns; for example, gay people take special risks of beatings while hitchhiking, and gay couples do not benefit from airline fare reductions which apply to heterosexual marriages. The list of concerns that can be generated in each cell is extensive.

To further complicate matters, imagine that for every institution and every movement there are social, political, psychological, economic, and environmental factors to consider. Now, what was a two-dimensional matrix becomes three-dimensional. That is how the complexity of the problem grows and that is why society is so hard to change.

If, however, we were able to learn the causes and goals of each of these separate liberation efforts, along with the kinds of decisions required in each of the separate institutions, we would be taking the first steps in the process of redesigning the American way of life.

All of us grew up believing that we needed to protect our way of life. Now we have come to realize that we need protection from it. Every social and ecological problem that America faces is at its root a problem reflecting our way of life, and can only be solved in the long run by its fundamental redesign.

The use of this matrix permits us to become aware of problems previously invisible to us, to see patterns emerge, to note overlapping and complementary situations that indicate where taking steps in behalf of one group would benefit another; for example, improving mobility for children would also improve mobility for older people. We would come to see that there are certain villains hiding and reappearing in each of the revolutions, the automobile, for instance. We would have a new appreciation for other oppressed peoples about whom we know little, for the great complexity of the problems we face, and for the many barriers to change.

We need such mechanisms to make the many invisible forces that shape our lives more visible to us. We need to take a good hard look at the way things work because for the first time in history we are in a situation where the kinds of problems we face cannot be solved by the actions of a few leaders but must be solved by everyone, all at once.

One cannot help but wonder what life would be like if children were to have a greater share of it. The temptation to create a scenario for the future based upon that possibility is almost irresistible. One could paint a glowing picture, but because we know that every utopia is also a dystopia and that every solution brings new problems, we must resist the temptation of utopian vision. It is nevertheless possible to examine the prospects for the liberation of children and some likely outcomes if changes were made. In so doing the first possibility to consider is that nothing will change. Maybe there will be no new national awareness of the predicament of children, no move for children's liberation. Even if there were, we can't be at all sure that it would be anything more than a change in consciousness, with no consequent change in institutions. Contrary to what one would like to believe, insight seldom leads to changes in behavior. Moreover, the best prediction of the future is what exists today. In spite of compelling analyses such as Alvin Toffler's *Future Shock,* which argue that changes in human relationships are not only increasing but accelerating, the best guess for the future of human affairs is still, as in forecasting the weather, that it will be more of the same.

With that admission out of the way, it is possible to look at some of the consequences which might come about should an effort for children's liberation succeed. Curiously, if there were positive changes we might not notice them because the problems are now largely invisible, making it impossible for us to see when the situation improves. We know so little about what constitutes progress that we just might not recognize it if it happened. Moreover, the changes would not happen overnight, and when they finally did it would seem to us that things certainly should have been this way all along. It would be something like making improvements in our environment: we only notice when the conditions are bad, we don't much notice when they get better because they are only returning to where they should have been anyway. Probably, if life were better for children, we would be more likely to notice first the negative consequences rather than positive ones, the difficulties of the transition period, the disruption of institutions, the jarring insults to our traditions and prejudices, the confusion as people try to adapt to new roles.

While looking for changes that would directly benefit children, we might miss the fact that many of the changes would indirectly benefit others, who might be able to take advantage of the changes more quickly. If we were to design more of our physical world to children's scale, for instance, most handicapped people would also be accommodated. Parents, especially women, would be benefited if various forms of alternative child care were available. Old people would find that a consciousness of ageism at the lower end of the age spectrum would lead to consciousness of ageism at the upper end. If the criminal justice system were made to fit both adults and children without a double standard, it would probably become more humane and efficient for adults. Ending censorship in magazines, films, and television would make it possible for adults to view material which they ae now denied because the fare must be graded down to children's level.

Then too, it is impossible to determine the effects of children's liberation on other liberation movements. Although children may not achieve such freedom soon, the effort may result in other groups being treated differently. Attempting to end paternalism for children may actually end it for other people.

We have seen this process work in a small way at the 1972 Democratic National Convention where for the first time there were large numbers of blacks, Chicanos, Indians and youth in attendance as delegates. One could argue that these groups would not have been represented in such large numbers had not the convention been pressured into dealing with an escalated problem, that of Women's Liberation. The women were a larger group and had the vote and the strength to make themselves heard at the convention. But it would have been impossible to bring women in without bringing in the other liberation groups that had previously made themselves visible. So by trying to solve the problems of one large group, we must as a matter of course solve the problems of other groups who might not have made it on their own. Perhaps that is to be our pattern of social change—continuing escalation to the concerns of larger groups. There are, after all, more women than blacks, more children than women, and more animals than children. Could it be that efforts to improve conditions for animals will be what is necessary to improve conditions for children?

This strategy of social change through escalation

to the concerns of larger numbers is similar to the organization consultant's effort to try to reduce conflict between departments not by bringing the warring parties together to discuss their differences, but by trying to get them committed to a superordinate goal, a goal that requires their cooperation for its solution. The conflict ends not because it was talked out but because it had to give way to a higher concern, that of achieving a shared goal. Children's liberation might have the same escalating effect.

Paradoxically, our concern for the plight of children comes not because our society has failed, but because it has succeeded. The kind of discontent that produces liberation movements is possible only when society develops the vision and strength to permit high-order concerns such as freedom, equality, and dignity to emerge. It is the success of our society which brings the high-level discontent that is the motivating force of any liberation movement.

Things often look worse when they are actually getting better. This is the history of revolutions. They start not when life is at its lowest ebb but when reforms have been instituted and the situation is improving. Only then do the people develop the strength and the consciousness of what they might have; it is this that enables them to build a revolution. It is the discrepancy between what people have and what they see that it is possible to have that causes dissatisfaction. This is why criticism and unrest are higher at the best campuses than at the worst ones; why racial tensions are greater where the most progress has been made; and why more good marriages fail than bad ones.[2] It is the age-old problem of rising expectations. People's needs are never fully satisfied because once one set of needs is met people simply move on to a higher set of needs. This only creates a new discontent, albeit of higher quality and most certainly preferable.

It may be, then, that the most we can expect from the liberation of children or from any positive social change is not peaceful satisfaction but a reduction in victimization followed by the development of high-level discontent. Perhaps the assessment of the quality and level of discontent engendered is the most realistic way of evaluating the success of any social program. We cannot therefore expect the number of problems of children to decrease, but we can expect that the problems would come to represent more humane concerns. That would be true for the parent-child relationship as well. The troubles will not end with children's liberation, for we simply trade the old oppressive problems in for new and more enlightened concerns.

Child psychologist Elaine Simpson points out a possible benefit to adults if children were liberated:

> Another very important effect would be enabling us all to relax from the effort at playing grown up all the time. By downgrading children we make it more dangerous to feel or

> behave as children ourselves—or whatever we project onto children in the way of feelings, inadequacies, dependencies, needs for physical contact, comforting, etc. The split between mind and body would be healed by reaccepting children into the mainstream of life. If we didn't have to pressure our children not to be children, we would join them in many ways we now envy them and deny ourselves.[3]

One outcome we can all hope for is that we adults will approach children with fewer burdensome responsibilities, with less guilt, less doubt, and less self-hate. Guilt and doubt, when coupled with feelings of responsibility which cannot be fully discharged, leave us with an attitude of vindictiveness toward children, and hatred toward ourselves.[4] If we can begin to move away from the need to reform children and begin to reform the situations in which we live together, we might come to like children more. Our first obligation is then to ourselves, to create the conditions under which we can like and respect our children. Perhaps the liberation of children will be such a condition and have such a consequence. But in truth we do not and cannot know ahead of time its possible effects. There is no way even to anticipate the many problems, let alone solve them. No guarantees come with children's liberation. But neither the promise of great benefits to all nor the prediction of great difficulties ahead can serve as the reason for granting or denying rights to children. Rights will be granted because without them children are incapacitated, oppressed, and abused. We don't yet know much about the way life should be for children, but we do know that the way it is now should not be.

When a child sees a person without a leg, he will point and ask. We wish he wouldn't. We wish he would learn to look away, as we have, and pretend there is nothing wrong.

Notes

Chapter 1

1. Among the more recent books dealing specifically with children's rights issues are:

Paul Adams, et al., *Children's Rights: Toward the Liberation of the Child* (New York: Praeger, 1971).

David Gottlieb, ed., *Children's Liberation* (Englewood Cliffs, N.J.: Prentice-Hall, 1973).

Youth Liberation of Ann Arbor, *Youth Liberation: News, Politics and Survival Information,* Youth Liberation of Ann Arbor, Michigan, 1972.

Mark Gerzon, *A Childhood for Every Child* (New York: Outerbridge and Lazard, Inc., 1973).

2. Shulamith Firestone, *The Dialectic of Sex* (New York: William Morrow and Co., Inc., 1970), p. 104.

3. See Rousseau's *Emile;* John Dewey's *Experience and Education;* Paul Goodman's, *Growing Up Absurd, Compulsory Miseducation,* and *A Community of Scholars;* Carl Rogers', *On Becoming a Person* and *Freedom to Learn;* A. S. Neill's *Summerhill;* Wilhelm Reich's, *The Function of the Orgasm* and *Character Analysis.*

4. Elain Simpson, unpublished paper, The University of California, Berkeley, February 21, 1972.

In another unpublished paper (June 3, 1973) she adds: "Actually little research seems to have had child liberation as a goal. One suspects that children are used for research for the same reasons that white rats and psychology students are. You don't have to pay them for their time and they don't ask too many embarrassing questions. Also, in the stressful academic atmosphere it is comforting to feel superior to at least someone. And no one will be critical if you indulge in a little speculation about how to manipulate and control them, whether they had best be indulged or treated firmly, whether to segragate them or refer them for counseling, whether one should reinforce this behavior or ignore that.

And from our place of vested interest as adults we can project onto children an image of carefree, irresponsible youth. We can feel a heartwarming tolerance as we observe their irrationality, egocentricity, suggestibility, impulsiveness, and dependence—traits that we ourselves have the decency to hide if we are aware of them in ourselves at all."

5. Bernard Apfelbaum, personal communication to the author, August 24, 1973.

Chapter 2

1. Philippe Aries, *Centuries of Childhood* (New York: Random House, Vintage Books, 1962).

Richard Howard, "Childhood Amnesia," *The Child's Part,* ed. Peter Brooks (Boston: Beacon Press, 1969), pp. 165-166.

J. H. Plumb, "The Great Change in Children," *Horizon* (Winter, 1971), pp. 5-13.

2. Aries, *Centuries of Childhood.*

3. Special dress for children did not appear until the seventeenth century and then applied only to the aristocratic classes.

4. J. H. Plumb, *Great Change.*

5. Aries, *Centuries of Childhood.*

6. Mary Ellen Goodman, *The Culture of Childhood* (New York: Columbia University, Teachers College Press, 1970).

7. *Ibid.*

8. The question often asked in connection with the current move-

ment in children's rights is, "What age children are you talking about?" This is purely a nineteenth- and twentieth-century question. It would not have been asked in an earlier century because the idea that different ages dictated differing capabilities was simply not a valid issue.

9. Shulamith Firestone, *Dialectic of Sex.*

Chapter 3

1. B. F. Skinner, *Beyond Freedom and Dignity* (New York: Knopf, 1971).

2. A. S. Neill, *Freedom–Not License!* (New York: Hart Publishing Co., 1966).

3. Victor Goertzel and Mildred George Goertzel, *Cradles of Eminence,* (Boston: Little, Brown and Company, 1962).

4. Haim G. Ginott, *Between Parent and Child* (New York: The Macmillan Company, 1965).

Chapter 4

1. *White House Conference on Children–Report to the President,* (Washington, D.C.: U.S. Government Printing Office, 1970).

2. Kempe, C. H., Silverman, S. N., Steele, B. F., Droegmueller, W., and Silver, H. K., "The Battered-Child Syndrome," *Journal of the American Medical Association,* 181 (July 7, 1962), pp. 17-24.

3. Serapio R. Zolba, "The Battered Child," *Science Digest* (December 1971) p. 8.

David G. Gil, *Violence Against Children* (Cambridge: Harvard University Press, 1970), p. 59.

4. David Bakan, *Slaughter of the Innocents* (San Francisco: Jossey-Bass, Inc., Publishers, 1971), p. 5.

5. *Ibid.*

6. Richard Sennett describes the problem this way: "This kind of family living in the suburbs surely is a little strange. Isn't the preference for suburbia as a setting for family life in reality an admission, tacit and unspoken to be sure, that the parents do not feel confident of their own human strengths to guide the child in the midst of an environment richer and more difficult than that of the neat lawns and tidy supermarkets of the suburbs? If a close, tight-knit

family emerges because the other elements of the adult and child world are made purposely weak, if parents assume their children will be better human beings for being shielded or deprived of society outside the home and homelike schools, surely the family life that results is a forced and unnatural intimacy." p. 36. Richard Sennett, "The Brutality of Modern Families," *Trans-action,* (September 1970), p. 36-37.

7. Leslie Y. and Karen Rabkin, "Children of the Kibbutz," *Psychology Today* (September, 1969), p. 46.

8. Urie Bronfenbrenner, *Two Worlds of Childhood: United States and U.S.S.R.* (New York: Russell Sage Foundation, 1970).

The Circulos, the child care collectives in Cuba based upon its co-operative predecessors the kibbutz in Israel and the children's collective in Russia is the most recent attempt to rationalize child care. The budget priority is high in this program (e.g. children snack on fresh oranges rather than cookies or crackers) and it is widely respected as an unusually successful venture.

Erik Erikson, *Childhood and Society* (New York: W. W. Norton, 1950).

Chapter 5

1. Kate Wiggins, *Children's Rights* (Boston: Houghton & Mifflin Co., Inc., 1892).

2. Edward M. Swartz, *Toys That Don't Care* (Boston: Gambit Publishing Co., 1971).

3. Marvin Kaye, *A Toy is Born* (New York: Stein and Day, Publishers, 1973).

4. Evelyn Sarson, "Action for Children's Television, the First National Symposium on the Effect on Children of Television Programming and Advertising," Discus-Avon Pub. Co., New York (1971).

5. *The Mental Health of the Child,* Program reports of the National Institute of Mental Health, Julius Segal, PhD, Editor, Program Analysis and Evaluation Branch, Office of Program Planning and Evaluation, National Institute of Mental Health. 5600 Fishers Lane, Rockville, Maryland, 20852 (June 1971), Public Health Service Publication No. 2168.

6. "In the discussion of urban design, childhood is commonly treated as a minor nuisance to be isolated in conveniently distributed play and study areas, or temporarily stored in the suburbs, out of the way of the more important members and activities of the adult community.

"This blatant disregard for the needs of the young could scarcely be more glaringly revealed than in a recent statement by an environmental engineer and an urban planner to the effect that 'nobody is really leaving the city . . . People never move beyond their functional and spiritual commuting radius.

"Beyond whose commuting radius? Beyond that of the exploring 5-year-old wanderer, or that of the 10-year-old at the wheel of his 100-horse-power automobile? At what age do we become people, and at what age do people cease to be the products of their childhood?" Albert Eide Parr, "To Make the City a Child's Milieu," *The New York Times* (Sunday, July 4, 1971).

Chapter 6

1. "I like to think that we respect our children's intelligence enough to suppose that the world need be presented to them in no rosy light . . . the world has not spared children hunger, cold, sorrow, pain, fear, loneliness, disease, death, war, famine, or madness. Why should we hesitate to make use of this knowledge when writing for them?" (John Neufeld, WLB, October, 1971).

2. Sheila Egoff, "If That Don't Do No Good, That Won't Do No Harm: The Uses and Dangers of Mediocrity in Children's Reading," *Library Journal* (October 15, 1972), p. 93.

3. Ann Kalkhoff, "Innocent Children or Innocent Librarians," *Library Journal* (October 15, 1972), p. 89.

4. Sunny Decker, *An Empty Spoon,* (New York: Harper & Row, Inc., 1970).

5. "What's New at School," CBS News Special (April 18, 1972).

6. David Goslin, *Guidelines for the collection, maintenance and dissemination of pupil records; report of a conference on the ethical and legal aspects of school record keeping,* Russell Sage Foundation at Sterling Forest Conference Center, New York (1969).

Chapter 7

1. Charles Siberman, *Crisis in the Classroom* (New York: Random House, 1970).

2. James Hearndon, *How to Survive in Your Native Land* (New York: Bantam Books, Inc., 1972).

3. George Gallup. *The George Gallup Poll 1935-1971* Vol. 2 (New York: Random House, 1972) p. 1353.

4. "The atmosphere of the home is prolonged in the school, where the students soon discover that (as in the home) in order to achieve some satisfaction they must adapt to the precepts which have been set from above. *One of these precepts is not to think.*" (Paolo Friere, *Pedagogy of the Oppressed* [New York: Herder & Herder, 1968], p. 151.)

5. John Holt, *Freedom and Beyond* (New York: E. P. Dutton & Co., Inc. 1972).

6. Ivan Illich, *De-Schooling Society* (New York: Harper & Row, 1970).

7. *Yellow Pages on Learning Resources,* Richard S. Wurman, Ed., Group for Environmental Education, Inc. (1972).

8. "A general state education is a mere contrivance for molding people to be exactly like one another; and as the mold in which it casts them is that which pleases the predominant power in the government—whether this be a monarch, a priesthood, an aristocracy, or the majority of the existing generation—in proportion as it is efficient and successful, it establishes a despotism over the mind, leading by natural tendency to one over the body." (John Stuart Mill)

9. George Dennison, *The Lives of Children* (New York: Random House, 1969).

Nat Hentoff, *Our Children Are Dying* (New York: The Viking Press, 1966).

John Holt, *Freedom and Beyond.*

Ivan Illich, *De-Schooling Society.*

James Hearndon, *The Way It Spozed To Be* (New York: Bantam Books, Inc., 1968).

Jonathan Kozol, *Free Schools* (Boston: Houghton Mifflin Co., Inc., 1972).

Paolo Friere, *Pedagogy of the Oppressed.*

10. Bertrand Russell, *Marriage and Morals* (New York: Liveright, 1951).

11. A more complete discussion of this can be found in: Margaret Mead, *Culture and Commitment* (New York: Natural History Press, Doubleday & Co., Inc., 1970).

Richard E. Farson, "The Reverse Transmission of Culture," *Experiences in Being,* ed., Bernice Marshall (Wadsworth Publishing Co., Inc., 1971), p. 214-219.

12. In "How We Learn Today in America," *Saturday Review,* (August 19, 1972), p. 33, Michael Rossman discusses prefigurative learning as a means by which youth will be able to choose alternative life-styles with the approval of their parents. "We are in for the age-democratization of society in general, and of education in particular. Already institutions of *post*-figurative learning have started to function "in reverse" as liberal professors learn new style and content from their students and kids turn on their families. Every wave of immigrants has learned in part from its children to adapt to a new culture. But we are all immigrants of Time now, arriving daily on the strange shores of the future; and the prefigurative capacities of the traditional family are as inadequate for our naturalization as are the co-figurative processes of the nuclear couple. Deeply different sorts of institutions must arise to incorporate these tendencies in new balance.

". . . the processes of prefigurative learning are by definition at the heart of the alternative system."

Chapter 8

1. John R. Seeley, "Corporal Punishment: Social Context and Sexual Overtones," *Sexual Behavior* Vol. 1 (April, 1971).

2. Alan Reitman, Judith Follman, Edward T. Ladd, *Corporal Punishment in the Public Schools: The Use of Force in Controlling Student Behavior,* ACLU Report (March, 1972), p. 34.

3. *Ibid.*, p. 3. A continuing number of references to this report have been made throughout the chapter.

4. Dr. Thomas Gordon, *Parent-Effectiveness Training: The "No-Lose" Program for Raising Responsible Children* (New York: Peter H. Wyden, Inc. 1970).

5. "If you strike a child, take care that you strike it in anger,

even at the risk of maiming it for life. A blow in cold blood neither can nor should be forgiven." (George Bernard Shaw, *Maxims for Revolutionists.*)

6. *Op. Cit.*, "Corporal Punishment: Social Context and Sexual Overtones."

7. David G. Gil, *Violence Against Children* (Cambridge, Massachusetts: Harvard University Press, 1970).

Chapter 9

1. Mary Breasted, *Oh! Sex Education!* (New York: The New American Library, Inc., 1971).

2. *Ibid.*

3. Haim G. Ginott, *Between Parent and Child* (New York: The Macmillan Company, 1965).

4. Dr. Benjamin Spock, *Baby and Child Care* (New York: Pocket Books, Inc., 1961).

5. The Guyon Society, based in Alhambra, California, advocates sexual freedom including adult-child sex at very early ages and claims a membership of approximately one thousand families representing most of the states.

6. "In Georgia one can receive a life imprisonment term upon being convicted of sodomy. In New York, when the partner is over eighteen years of age and has consented, the maximum sentence is one year. However, when the partner has not consented, a sentence of twenty years is possible.

"Every state has a statute prohibiting incest. The penalty varies from one year's imprisonment to fifty years' imprisonment. Some states impose fines up to two thousand dollars."

(Lars Ullerstam, *The Erotic Minorities* [New York: Grove Press, Inc., 1966].)

7. "Here the Kinsey Report confirms the early findings of Havelock Ellis, Sigmund Freud and others. Human sexuality is not a phenomenon which makes its appearance in puberty and/or during adolescence, it is rather clearly visible during infancy and early childhood. Not only can infants and very small children experience sexual stimulation, they can and do experience orgasms as well. A sexual experience takes place in many forms, homosexual, heterosexual,

voyeuristic, exhibitionistic, oral, anal and so on." (Edward M. Brecher, *The Sex Researchers,* [Boston: Little, Brown and Co., 1969].)

8. Alfred C. Kinsey, et al, *Sexual Behavior in the Human Female* (New York: W. P. Saunders, 1953), p. 103.

9. "One area of continuing social concern is sexual contact between children and adults. Very little physical harm was reported in these contacts. The Kinsey Reports note 'We have only one clean-cut case of serious injury done to a child.' " (Brecher, *Sex Reseachers).*

10. John Woodbury, Ph.D., and Elroy Schwartz, *The Silent Sin,* (New York: The New American Library, Inc., 1971).

11. Christopher Bagley, "Incest Behavior and Incest Taboo," *Social Problems*, Vol. 16, No. 4 (Spring 1969).

12. *Ibid.*

13. Karl Meninger, *Love Against Hate* (New York: Harcourt, Brace & World, Inc., 1942), p. 284.

Lauretta Bender and Abram Blau, "The Reaction of Children to Sexual Relations with Adults," *American Journal of Orthopsychiatry,* Vol. 7, (1937), pp. 500-518.

14. Germaine Greer, "Seduction is a Four-Letter Word," *Playboy* (January 1972), p. 82.

Chapter 10

1. Laurance S. Smith, "How Civilization Breeds Increased Juvenile Crime," *Los Angeles Times*, February 18, 1973, Part VII, p. 3.

2. The child labor amendment was introduced as a joint resolution by Senator Medill McCormick of Illinois and Congressman Israel M. Foster of Ohio. The resolution was approved by a vote of 297 to 69 in the House on April 24, 1924, and 61 to 23 in the Senate on June 2, 1924, but was never ratified by the states.

3. According to the 1870 Census, about one out of every eight children were employed. By 1900 approximately 1,750,000 children, or one out of six, were gainfully employed. 60 percent were agricultural workers; of the 40 percent in industry over half were children of immigrant families. By 1899, twenty eight states had passed some legislation regarding child labor. The laws ordinarily applied only to manufacturing and generally set the minimum age limit at twelve. A few states, however, had raised the working age to thirteen or fourteen.

4. Daniel Moynihan, *The Politics of the Guaranteed Annual Income* (New York: Random House, 1972).

Milton Friedman, *Capitalism & Freedom* (Chicago: The University of Chicago Press, 1962).

Chapter 11

1. There is another possible explanation. In England, children of the aristocracy inherited the property of their parents' estates at nineteen, but it took two years for the legal transfer of property rights during the eighteenth century. This may have resulted in the twenty-one-year-old age restriction on contracts and valid signature that exists today.

2. Avrum Stroll, "Censorship, Models and Self-Government," *The Journal of Value Inquiry*, Vol. 1, No. 2 (Fall 1967) The Hague, Netherlands: Nijhoff Pub., p. 81.

3. There are a number of children's lobbies, varying in their effectiveness to influence legislation. Two of the better known ones are the California Children's Lobby in Sacramento and the National Children's Lobby in Washington, D.C.

4. Child advocacy is becoming an important new field for both laymen and professionals. Larry Cole, in his book *Our Children's Keepers* (New York: Grossman, 1972), p. 130, suggests that self-appointed people form a new discipline, requiring certificates, in which they could function as professional parents, specialists in the care, education, development and protection of children. For a more complete discussion of the problems and possibilities in child advocacy see, *Child Advocacy, Report of a national baseline study,* Alfred J. Kahn, Sheila B. Kamerman, Bruce G. McGowan, Child Advocacy Research Project, Columbia University School of Social Work.

5. Clinton Rossiter describes this philosophy in the following way: "Government in a free state is properly the concern of all those who have a 'common interest with, and an attachment to the community.' The right to vote, as well as to hold office, should be limited to men who have an evident 'stake-in-society'—first, because they alone can make competent, responsible, uncorrupted judgments; second, because they alone have a clear right to consent to laws regulating or restricting the use of property." (Clinton Rossier, *Seedtime of the Republic* [New York: Harcourt, Brace & World, Inc., 1953].)

Chapter 12

1. Shulamith Firestone, *The Dialectic of Sex.*

2. "An Act to regulate the treatment and control of dependent, neglected and delinquent children, 1899." "The words delinquent child shall include any child under the age of sixteen years who violates any law of this state or any City or Village ordinance." The Country's first juvenile court law, Illinois, 1899. Robert H. Bremner, *Children and Youth in America,* Volume II; 1866-1932 (Cambridge: Harvard University Press, 1971).

3. In 92 percent of the Children's Court hearings in New York counsel is not present to participate in its proceedings.

4. Howard James, *Children In Trouble: A National Scandal* (New York: David McKay Company, Inc., 1970), pp. 71-72.

5. Laurance S. Smith, "How 'Civilization' Breeds Increased Juvenile Crime," *Los Angeles Times* (February 18, 1973), Part VII, p. 3.

6. Ramsey Clark, *Crime in America* (New York: Simon and Schuster, Inc., 1970), pp. 40-41.

7. Albert D. Biderman and Raymond Bauer, *Social Indicators and Goals* (Cambridge: M.I.T. Press, 1966).

8. Ramsey Clark, *Crime.*

9. Osborn Segerberg, Jr., "Watch Out For The Mini-Muggers," *New York Magazine* Vol. 3., No. 2. (January 12, 1970).

10. This statement also appears in a discussion of a similar problem in Nat Hentoff, "Why Students Want Their Constitutional Rights," *Saturday Review* (May 22, 1971).

Chapter 13

1. ". . . being a child tends to mean mostly that one is unable to act in certain ways. Thus, childhood itself may be viewed as a form of 'disability.' " (Thomas S. Szasz, *The Myth of Mental Illness* (New York: Harper and Row, 1961), p. 244.

2. See the author's articles, "How Can Anything That Feels So Bad Be So Good," *Saturday Review* (September 6, 1969), p. 20, and "Why Good Marriages Fail," *McCall's* (October 1971).

3. Elaine Simpson, in a personal communication to the author, April 24, 1973.

4. "Self-doubts many adults have concerning their own legitimacy lead to an enormous vindictiveness toward the young . . ." ("The Young are Captives of Each Other: A Conversation with David Riesman and T. George Harris," *Psychology Today* [October 1969]).

Index

Farson, Richard Evans, 1926-.

Birthrights

DATE			
SEP 2 3 1975			
NOV 9 1976			
JUL 1 9 1977			
FEB 2 7 1979			
OCT 2 7 198			
MAR 2 1982			
MAR 2 9 1982			
AUG 1 0 1998			